Gandhi the Pacifist

Gandhi the Pacifist

K. Srinivas

Suryodaya Books
New Delhi

Cataloging in Publication Data – DK
[Courtesy: D.K. Agencies (P) Ltd. <docinfo@dkagencies.com>]

Srinivas, K. (Kunchapudi), 1955-

Gandhi the pacifist / K. Srinivas.

p. cm.
Includes bibliographical references and index.
ISBN 13: 9788192570228

1. Gandhi, Mahatma, 1869–1948 – Philosophy.
2. Pacifists – India – Biography. 3. Statesmen – India – Biography. 4. Peace. I. Title.

DDC 954.035 23

ISBN 13: 978-81-925702-2-8
First published in India in 2015

Printed and published by:
Suryodaya Books
"Suryodaya", D-36/A-1, Mohan Garden
Najafgarh Road
New Delhi – 110 059
Phone (011) 2535 3435

Distributed by:
D.K. Printworld (P) Ltd.
Regd. Office: *Vedasri*, F-395, Sudarshan Park
(Metro Station: Ramesh Nagar)
New Delhi – 110 015
Phones: (011) 2545 3975, 2546 6019; *Fax*: 2546 5926
e-mail: indology@dkprintworld.com
Web: www.dkprintworld.com

To

Professor Vempati Kutumba Sastry

Preface

So much is written and discussed on Gandhian thought since 1950s. Knowing very well that Gandhi is no more a fertile area I undertook this venture of publishing some of my reflections on Gandhian thought concerning his robust idealism and its relevance to contemporary times. I personally feel that the very survival of Gandhian thought establishes the fact that it is not a rigid set of doctrines to be read as a fairytale but has inbuilt elasticity to be practised by the generations of people for the preservation of life and society. The present work is an attempt to highlight the central doctrines of Gandhian idealism and their impact on human societies. We must keep in mind that no philosophical doctrine is foolproof or immune to revision. Every philosophical doctrine is susceptible to criticism. In that sense, Gandhian idealism is not an exception to this rule.

Of course, the changing social and political circumstances necessitate a radical shift in our ideologies too. The contemporary developments in the realm of science and technology ushered in new human relations and values. Also, we are witnessing lopsided development of societies all over the globe which deprives certain privileges to a section of people. The gap between the rich and poor is widening day by day. The economic and social imbalances rob people of their human dignity. The supremacy of machine over man gradually transformed human condition into a state of despair. To resurrect human race from such a state of despair there is a need to revitalize human values. The life without human values is like a ship drifting in the mid-sea without a pilot or a helmsman. Human values guide us through the difficult situations. A welfare society worth the name cannot afford to ignore the existence of human values. The ideal of any welfare society is to fulfil the basic needs of people and to protect their fundamental rights. Gandhi time and again reminded us of the importance of human values.

Gandhi's philosophy of action is a direct outcome of his faith in the teachings of *Bhagavad-Gītā*. But his philosophy of action is based on the principle of nonviolence (*ahiṁsā*) which is not only extended to one's deeds but also to thought and speech. Thus Gandhi can be befittingly called a radical pacifist. The influence of Christianity, Buddhism, and Jainism are also conspicuous on Gandhi. He admired and assimilated what is best in other religious faiths without alienating from his own Hindu faith. Nonviolence, compassion, and love must be part of our social actions, according to Gandhi. But these virtues cannot be solely expressed in the individual's actions but must also reflect in the social and political life of individuals. An individual as a moral agent cannot live like a recluse. Every individual's life is entangled with the life of community, society, nation, and humanity. Throughout his life Gandhi tried to bring both individual and social spheres together for it is a contradiction in terms to call someone individually good and socially bad, and socially good and individually bad. Gandhi thought that India would be a right nation where he can experiment with his ideals successfully. As an Indian he knew the mentality of his fellow Indians and their faith in the scriptures.

Another important factor to be highlighted is that like Socrates, Gandhi always respected his inner voice (conscience). By and large, all his actions are guided by his inner voice. He firmly believed that the three methods of action — nonviolence, compassion, and love — are the only legitimate means to establish peace and harmony in family and communal relationships, internal politics of nation, and international relationships. Gandhi never deviated from his path and even went to an extent of threatening his followers that he would retire to forest if they did not shun hatred and violence. Perhaps Gandhi was lucky enough to have trusted and disciplined followers. The confidence in his followers made Gandhi to challenge even Hitler to face his unarmed army of nonviolent, compassionate, and loving souls if he invaded India. Of course, these challenges of Gandhi make us think that Gandhi was daydreaming.

Gandhi's philosophy of action manifested in his practice of *satyāgraha.* It is often interpreted as "passive resistance" or "nonviolent resistance" or "civil disobedience". But Gandhi did not mean any of these things. They are only corollaries or aspects or results of *satyāgraha,* which means "passionate adherence to truth". Truth being the law and support of the universe cannot be ignored by any individual. Nonviolence and compassion are the two aspects of Truth. There are believers and non-believers in the existence of God, but there is none who can deny the existence of Truth. This is the reason why Gandhi equated God with Truth. Disobedience of civil laws, which spread evil, is also a kind of resistance. Truly speaking resistance is not passive. With love and nonviolence, Gandhi held, we can transform our deadliest enemies into good friends. The application of the robust idealism of Gandhi to social, political, and international fields is not an easy affair. It certainly requires many provisos and adjustments. At the end of the British rule Gandhi realized that his robust idealism can be practised only at individual level.

Gandhi alone could truly practise what was upheld by him. Unfortunately the pragmatic world in which we live is not what Gandhi thought it to be. The limitations imposed on the effectiveness of Gandhian idealism only speak about the kind of reality that we face today. Poverty, illiteracy, and lack of proper health care are of great concern to every nation. Greed, dishonesty, degenerated moral system, and lack of commitment to social duties deprive human beings of their dignity. There is no doubt Gandhian idealism offers great hope to humanity.

The present work contains seven chapters. The seventh chapter is a book review. I chose to include it in the present work as the author, Ram Chandra Pradhan, in his book *Reading and Reappraising Gandhi* provides us with an overview of Gandhian idealism and the ways in which it was interpreted.

I express my deep sense of gratitude to Prof. K. Ramakrishna Rao, formerly Chairman of Indian Council of Philosophical Research (ICPR), New Delhi, and currently Chancellor of GITAM University, Visakhapatnam, for encouraging me to write on Gandhian thought by extending invitation to take part in the national and international seminars held in the Centre for Gandhian Studies at GITAM and for Gandhirama in New Delhi. My interaction with Gandhian scholars made me realize the significance of Gandhian thought today. Also, I sincerely thank Prof. Christine Chojnacki, Chairman, Centre for Indian Culture at Jean Moulin University at Lyon 3, France, for extending me an invitation as visiting professor. The interest evinced by the faculty and students of Jean Moulin University on Gandhi compelled me to pen down my reflections on Gandhian thought. I cannot forget the moral support extended by my friends Prof. S. Pannirselvame, Dean, School of Humanities, Pondicherry University, and Dr Clement Lourdes, Associate Professor, Department of English, Pondicherry University, while pursuing the present project.

Puducherry **K. Srinivas**
July 2014

Contents

Preface *vii*

1. Prologue 1
2. Peace as an Embodiment of Spirituality 24
3. Conflict Resolution 33
4. Corruption and Human Values 47
5. Economic Philosophy 60
6. Socialist Outlook: Gandhi and Marx 75
7. Reappraising Gandhi 88

Epilogue 113

Bibliography 116

Index 119

1

Prologue

MOHANDAS Karamchand Gandhi (1869–1948) is regarded as one of the most acknowledged pacifists of the twentieth century. He not only has admirers within the Indian subcontinent, but also all over the globe. Both people and organizations were influenced by the Gandhian ideals in one way or the other. One of the contemporary debates is whether Gandhi can be considered a philosopher at all. Of course, in the sense in which we consider Plato and Śaṅkara as philosophers, we cannot consider Gandhi as one for he never attempted to work out a systematic philosophy of his own. I consider Gandhi more a *karmayogī* than a *dārśanika* for he aimed at practising what he believed in as an ideal. Thus he had a world-view of his own; but his philosophy of action often obfuscated his world-view. In fact, what passes in the name of Gandhian philosophy today is culled out from his life and action by his followers. What is typical of Gandhi is that he shared many characteristics with the ancient and later Indian sages and seers, and what interests us about these great Indian sages and seers is that they did not systematically work out any metaphysics or epistemology, but they evolved a view of life and reality which transcended our discursive thought. A strict philosophical standpoint, especially in the occidental traditions, demands rigidity and certainty concerning any world-view. But this is not the case with the oriental philosophical traditions where a world-view evolves out of intuition and insightfulness. The great sages and seers of the past discovered the eternal truths of life not by employing any rigorous logical methods. One who closely observed Gandhi's life would certainly realize that Gandhi's world-view is the outcome of his own intuition and insightfulness. Thus his method is in no way different from the method of those great sages and seers. It is a mistake to think that all our actions are always guided by reason. Pure reason, as aptly remarked by the German idealist Immanuel Kant, has its limitations too. It is our practical reason which guides us in the matters concerning freedom, morality and religion. Therefore, formal reason cannot be treated as the only paradigm of human life. It is the practical reason that sets forth certain ideals of life which regulate our human relationships. Gandhian philosophy is laced with so much of philosophical idealism because humans alone can practise ideals. This does not mean Gandhi opposed rational approach to human life. Certainly reason has its own role to play in our day-to-day dealings with fellow humans. As a humanist Gandhi envisaged a world-view wherein all human beings enjoy equal freedom, justice and happiness.

Sometimes it is difficult for the people of present generation to provide a dispassionate account of Gandhian philosophy. The political and social scenario when Gandhi appeared on the Indian scene was completely different. Although there was a literate minority which was politically conscious; yet the majority of illiterate people were not politically active. They silently suffered disease, hunger, poverty and humiliation during the British rule. Gandhi's appearance on the scene drastically changed the mindset of people of all ages irrespective of their educational and social backgrounds. It was a miracle that young and old, men and women became politically enthusiastic. Gandhi infused hope into their despair by becoming a beacon. Those who were closely associated with Gandhi refused to detach themselves from the thought and life of Gandhi. It may be easier for the people of present generation to demarcate between the emotional and intellectual life and teachings of Gandhi, but it is not possible for those who were closely associated with him to do so. For them Gandhianism includes thought, feeling, emotion and action. There is no watertight distinction among those elements. They are fused into one. This makes Gandhi an enigma.

One has to make a distinction between the fundamental principles of Gandhi's thought and his practices. The fundamental principles of Gandhian thought have universal appeal in the sense that they are beyond space and time. They are like Kant's Categorical Imperative. They are applicable to all the generations of individuals. But some of his practices and programmes were specific to his time. Such a distinction between Gandhian thought and his practices may appear to be heretical, for we often get confused between principles and practices. We give equal importance to both. In our day-to-day life we do come across a number of individuals imitating Gandhi's mannerisms thinking that such a practice would enable them to enter into the spirit of Gandhian thought. But the irony is that Gandhi never claimed to be a Gandhian for he was always prepared to modify his views to meet the demands of a new situation. Thus he was a hardcore pragmatist. What is interesting to notice is that some of Gandhi's programmes were not tested sufficiently and many of his programmes were found wanting in many respects. Had Gandhi not met his unnatural death in 1948 he would have certainly changed some of his strategies and practices. But his fundamental principles always remained the same and have had lasting influence on many great social reformers all over the globe.

There is perceivable simplicity in Gandhian thought. His idealism is combined with his pragmatic outlook to deal with social problems. But one can also notice some sort of mysticism in his mental make-up. This often resulted in inconsistencies in Gandhi's thought and action. It is not all that easy for a Gandhian to defend Gandhi for he never hesitated to deviate from what he said before if situation demanded a new strategy. As an outright pragmatist Gandhi did not see anything wrong with that. His autobiography *My Experiments with Truth* is a testimony to this fact. He allowed the world of reality to make its impact on his own life in order to reach its demands. At times, one feels that though Gandhi claimed to be simple it is difficult to understand his complex personality. This is because Gandhi aimed to achieve simplicity in thought, action, attitude and approach to life. He considered life in its totality and his responses to life involved certain amount of complicatedness which people could not understand. For Gandhi, simplicity is the ideal of life and his followers mistook it for poverty and extolled it. But poverty is a sin and it has evil effects on the individual and society. The food eaten by Gandhi and the cloths worn by Gandhi were simple but rich in quality.

Gandhi's simplicity made him realize that the essence of all great religions is the same. The basic unity of all religions can be realized only when we make their practices simple. According to him, all the differences among the great religions of the world surface only when we make their practices complex and complicated. We have to discard this complexity in order to identify ourselves with the Supreme. Complexity makes religions a divisive force. It is the simplicity that makes religions a unifying force. Gandhi being an ordinary man is not really endowed with extraordinary traits. He was born in an ordinary family and was physically not very impressive. His appearance in South Africa made him an unusual personality with impeccable moral qualities. He was a stoic. He endured pain and suffering to achieve what he wanted to achieve as a moral being. Thus Gandhi was an ordinary person with an extraordinary yearning for establishing equality and justice. He became a symbol of purity, goodness and excellence for millions of Indians who were struggling for their basic survival needs during the British rule.

To be a normal person is something difficult. Gandhi made himself to be a normal person through his will and endeavour even in the most difficult times. This is something extraordinary to remain normal consistently. We, as ordinary human beings, hardly possess this extraordinary skill to remain always normal and composed because of our wavering mind. This makes Gandhi a unique personality. However, we need to be cautious in giving this blanket testimonial to Gandhi, for Gandhi too committed many Himalayan blunders. But his noble deeds and his concern for humanity obfuscate these Himalayan blunders. As an apostle of peace he never wanted to see bloodshed. Of course, it is not all that easy to imitate Gandhi, but one can make an effort. Another interesting thing about Gandhi is that he never advised others to do what he himself could not do.

Gandhianism is blended with extreme form of philosophical idealism. This is evident from Gandhi's belief that there is innate capacity in every human being to respond to noble impulses. In the West the doctrine of innate ideas was criticized by John Locke, but was proved to be true by the philosophers like Noam Chomsky. Perhaps this innate capacity to grasp what is worthy of emulation makes human species far superior to any other living species. Every individual must allow his/her conscience to judge what is right and what is wrong. One's will is certainly subordinate to one's conscience. One should not allow one's will to dominate one's conscience for the acts of the former are selfish and the acts of the latter are desirable, hence altruistic. Gandhi expected highest form of moral conduct from every individual. Gandhi's personal interaction with his companions raised their moral standards. He overcame one weakness after another through his sincere effort and endeavour. He asked his companions to do the same.

Gandhi's own experience towards life fashioned his attitude to social change. He believed that it is through self-discipline one can bring about social change that would benefit the entire community of individuals. Gandhi's life is an open book in the sense that he never concealed anything, including his weaknesses from others. He shared his personal experiences with his companions. The reason is that Gandhi believed that truth is the great cleanser. When an individual strives for truth he shares in an attribute of God. This conviction made Gandhi hold the view that "Truth is God". Since every man possesses divinity within himself he is capable of rising to greater heights with necessary conviction and effort. To Gandhi, the change in society presupposes the change in the individual first. Not only that, Gandhi was an optimist. When Gandhi arrived in India the people of India were already experiencing the colonial rule of the British. But he was optimistic in changing the life of millions of people in India.

The Western civilization infused hope and optimism into the minds of people all over the world through its scientific and technological advancement. On the one hand, it aimed that science and technology would take care of material comforts of the individuals, and on the other hand, education and social reforms would take care of all other social problems. In this sense the eighteenth and nineteenth centuries were an era of great hope to humanity. The enormous expansion in knowledge, wealth and comfort, the increasing mastery and control over disease and famine, the gradual conquest of physical and natural obstacles gave humanity the faith in education, science and technology. They believed that science and technology would certainly transform the scope of the world. Such a belief was further propelled by the faith in the power of social forces and legislation to change human nature. Karl Marx was one of the adherents of this view. He held that changes in the production forces would necessitate changes in the production relations. Individual's attitude and character would be transformed by such production relations. Thus Marx emphasized more on economic base which determines the scope of superstructure. The social change will necessarily bring about the change in individual himself.

Leo Tolstoy and Henry David Thoreau influenced Gandhi a lot. Both these philosophers stressed the significance of individual and his responsibility towards social construction. As Aristotle held one cannot think of an individual without society and vice versa. Similarly, the great scriptures of all the great religions of the world have had their lasting influence on Gandhi. Both the *Bible* and the *Gītā* gave so much importance to individual. In fact, every religion says that of all the births the human birth is so precious. Humans are capable of introspection and remorsefulness. They alone can understand the feelings and the sufferings of the fellow human beings. According to Gandhi, an individual has a bigger role to play in transforming the society. Without social reforms society is like a stagnant pond breeding reptiles. Any social reform presupposes reform in the individual.

Struggle for the political freedom of India and the struggle for social emancipation of the downtrodden were two important struggles that occupied the entire life of Gandhi. His undaunted faith in innate human goodness made him believe that political freedom of India could be achieved without any violence by convincing the British. In fact, Gandhi viewed that the political freedom of Indian people would be necessary not only for the well-being of Indian people, but also for the people of Britain. The subjugation of Indian people by the British harmed both the sides. The people of India developed servile mentality like Nietzsche's Dionysians and the British became the bullies or masters like his Apollonians. Such an attitude towards the people of India by the British affected the social life of the people of Britain. One cannot be a tyrant in India and a democrat in his own country. Therefore, liberation of India from the British is the only way for the Britain to be a full-fledged democracy.

Among other things, Gandhi had passion for Hindu society and its cherished values. He did not oppose modernism, but wanted modern values to be incorporated into traditional value system. He held tradition with high esteem. Modernization is based on tradition. What is contemporary is created on top of the past. Our natural languages and laws of the land are the best examples for that. We simply improve upon those aspects of life which already exist in our social structure. Without tradition modernity becomes a misnomer. The coexistence of tradition and modernity balances human value system. Such an exercise would benefit both the traditional Hindu value system and modernity without giving up any one of them. One should not change one's faith. Change in one's faith is the symbol of personal deterioration. One can admire and accept any religious faith other than one's own without alienating from his/her own faith. According to Gandhi, the essence of all religions is the same. But our different religious practices make them appear as if the essence of one religious faith is completely opposed to the essence of another. But it is not really the case. Gandhi also opposed religious conversions. If the essence of all religions is one and the same, then what is the need for one to convert from one religious faith to another?

Gandhi's faith in the individual made him change those aspects of Hindu life that prevented the complete flowering of an individual's personality. He wanted political freedom for the people of India for otherwise the people of India cannot enjoy their individual freedom in such a hostile atmosphere.

Also, such an atmosphere does not allow individuals to exhibit their natural talents as they are under constant external pressure. This will also demand far-reaching economic and social changes. Once these preconditions are met with the individuals through self-discipline, effort and endeavour change themselves into integrated personalities. A society of integrated personalities is a society that enjoys freedom and justice. This was a dream of Gandhi and he had great faith in his dream to become true.

Gandhi was a fearless person. His fearlessness resembles that of the great ancient Greek philosopher, Socrates. The latter refused to admit that what he taught to his disciples was untruth. Instead he was prepared to take the deadly poison without deviating from the path of truth. What Socrates and Gandhi shared with each other is that they never led the life of cowardice. Gandhi advised his companions to nurture this ideal of fearlessness. An integrated personality, he claimed, is fearless. We fear something or somebody only when we are houses divided within us. Fear is the outcome of our inner contradictions. We need to harmonize different aspects of our life to be an integrated personality. Gandhi echoes Sri Aurobindo in this respect. An individual who is afraid of something or somebody either generates fear or anger in others. A fearless person is always respected in the community of individuals. When we are afraid of an animal the animal becomes more and more aggressive sensing our pulse.

Although Gandhi was physically weak he was morally a courageous person. Gandhi spent his life in South Africa during 1893–1914. Once when he returned to South Africa from India he was advised by the people not to travel as there may be a racial attack on him. But he was very stubborn and continued his journey to South Africa only to be beaten up by the racists. What is remarkable of Gandhi was that he did not want to forgo his rights just because of aggression by others. His nightmare experiences in South Africa did not deter him from undertaking another trip to the same country to help the suppressed community of individuals in that country to make them realize their rights. Thus even death was afraid of Gandhi's fearlessness. He sufficiently experimented on fearlessness and asked his companions to adhere to this ideal. In 1920s the very idea of jail would shatter one's confidence, but Gandhi appealed to his fellow countrymen to participate in the non-cooperation movement against the British government and ready to face the jail fearlessly. Surprisingly, thousands of men and women responded to the clarion call given by Gandhi. Slowly Gandhi made people to face the fear of loss of property as well as life. The point here is that Gandhi could successfully instil fearlessness in the minds of people. Then in 1930s people participated in large numbers in many struggles and finally for the struggle for freedom with fearlessness. This made Gandhi a very successful mass leader. Of course, there were many people who resisted the call given by Gandhi and behaved against the wishes of Gandhi. But the behaviour of a small section of people did not deter Gandhi from going ahead with his mission.

From fearlessness Gandhi moved to love. Generally we are afraid of those things which we do not know. It is the sense of strangeness that alienates us. We are afraid of darkness for we cannot see anything. Even the things known to us appear to be different in darkness. Light alone can help us in dispelling the darkness. If darkness causes fear in us, light instils fearlessness. What we know through our senses belongs to us. When we come to know other individuals there arises a sense of kinship with them. This sense of kinship, felt Gandhi, is due to the divinity of God which all of us share. Every individual possesses noble qualities and inherent talents. Only when we know people in their true character then only we start loving them. Thus, for Gandhi, our feeling of kinship is based on love.

Fearlessness and love made Gandhi closer to every human being that he encountered in his life. The divinity that he saw within himself he found in others too. There is no substitute for love to cement our personal relationships with others. Thus Gandhi taught his fellowmen how to shun hatred in all forms. Yet, it is a mistake to think that he could eradicate the sense of fear and hatred fully. Exceptions are always there and these exceptions remain as minority. This paved the way for Gandhi to establish his mission of nonviolence. Although we fought the British we as Indians still maintain friendship and cooperation with Britain even today. India is a member of the Commonwealth of Nations (formerty British Commonwealth). The credit must go to Gandhi for inculcating the sense of forgiveness in the Indian minds. As he said violence breeds further violence. Hatred and conflicts would destroy both the sides involved in conflicts. When someone asked Gandhi about the future Indo-British relations he replied that it all depends upon the way in which the problem between the two nations was resolved. If the problem was resolved through violence and animosity then there exist no relations. If the problem was solved amicably then the people of both the nations would remain as good friends helping each other's cause. Thus Gandhi is remembered not only in India but all over the globe for spreading the ideal of nonviolence. Even the United Nations owes something to this great Gandhian ideal.

Let us now see how Gandhi reposed his unquestioned faith in God. Faith in God is something internal for him. Certainly it was not the result of imaginative vision or analytical thought. Like many others Gandhi tried to advance arguments why he believed in God. It was something that he accepted instinctively when he was young and carried on throughout his life. God was a fundamental fact in life for Gandhi and the world of reality is His gift. And this gift of God has a physical order, and is a moral one. It is spiritual in character and is governed by values which are above all the empirical matters. This spiritual character of the world is something that Gandhi accepted without any question although he had sufficient reasons to believe in it. God for Gandhi was an immediate datum of consciousness. Since the world is governed by a moral order it is possible to commune with it. Man being part and parcel of this moral order (*ṛta*) does possess this spiritual nature. Therefore, Gandhi drew the conclusion that there can be communication between the spirit of man and the spirit of nature. Gandhi arrived at such a conclusion not through any logical inference but through his immediate fact of experience. One finds some sort of mystic element in Gandhi's thought when he talked about his inner voice through which he communed with God. Sometimes he considered God as personality and at time he called God the source of his inner voice. In his difficult times Gandhi relied more on his inner voice than other forms of human thought and reaction.

When Gandhi made some statements about God they appear to be inconsistent with each other. This is the case with all mystics. Gandhi being a mystic is not an exception to this rule. He experienced the infinitude and power of the ultimate. But when he wanted to narrate his experience Gandhi failed to do so for our finite language cannot capture the Infinite, hence we find a lot of inconsistencies in his expressions about God. Further Gandhi made a distinction between religion and religious practices. Religion is the faith in Supreme Reality which sums up all our experiences and in this sense religion is one and the same for all. But religious practices deal with the broader aspects of such experience. Thus the practices of one religious faith may differ from the other. But all religious practices aim at the same Supreme Reality in spite of apparent differences among them. According to Gandhi, the experience of the Supreme cannot be broken up into pieces for it is a total complete experience of that power or being. Recognition of love is the basic human characteristic for Gandhi. In a way he identifies Love, Truth and God with each other although he called "God is Truth". Subsequently he modified this statement into "Truth is God". His argument is that the atheists may not believe in God, but they have respect for truth. If truth is identified with God then both theists and atheists pursue truth alike and by identifying truth with God Gandhi opined that we can cut across the differences between theists and atheists. This approach of Gandhi is akin to that of Descartes. The latter employed the doubting method to doubt everything that can be doubted. But he did not doubt the very existence of doubt. But he arrived at the "First Principle" of philosophy (*cogito ergo sum*) only through his doubting method. Similarly, Gandhi held that we must believe in the truth of our statement.

Gandhi's politics was based on traditional value system. Partly it was religious too. This is primarily the reason that made him attract the attention of the Indian masses. Religion for them is more precious than any other thing. They gave utmost importance to traditional human values. Although religion in its abstract sense is same for one and all, it differs from community to community in terms of religious practices. Unfortunately Gandhi in his use of religion as a motivating factor in politics could not maintain the distinction between religion and religious practices. His programmes heavily drew upon his own religious practices. Thus they had greater appeal to those who believed in the same religious practices. But those who did not follow similar religious practices got alienated from Gandhi's programmes. Gandhi could not escape from such a situation for he attempted to give concrete form to an abstract principle. Of course, Gandhi had great respect for other religions and was inspired by their teachings too.

Gandhi's programme of nonviolence is the outcome of his doctrine of love and truth. Perhaps, Gandhi thought that given the situation in which people of India were living in order to succeed against the mighty British Empire there cannot be any other way except resorting to nonviolent method. The non-cooperation with the British authorities would be the only peaceful approach to express people's disapproval. Gandhi successfully made use of religion and traditional values to justify his course of action against the British. He firmly believed that nonviolence is natural to man since it is the law of the human species. Darwin's survival of the fittest theory is applicable to only animals where might is right. The stronger animal dominates the weaker. But man defies the animal law as a moral agent. Nonviolence differentiates man from rest of the animal species. Nonviolence, for Gandhi, is the expression of natural justice. The actions of animals are based on instincts and impulses whereas men guide their actions through rationality. Gandhi made a distinction between the world of nature and the world of men. The former is subjected to the law of the survival of the fittest but the latter sees to that that even the weaker gets an opportunity to survive and progress.

Nonviolence being the expression of human nature it can be practised by only those who have strong willpower. It involves toughest decision-making on the part of the individual based on the situation that he/she faces and also on personal conviction. If these factors are missing then it is nonviolence but acquiescence. When we passively offer ourselves to any superior force then it is not nonviolence, according to Gandhi. Nonviolence is a path which we choose knowing fully the consequences resulting from such an act, because we consider such an act is the only right act. *Satyāgraha* or nonviolence is based on moral force. Being an expression of strength nonviolence is always a programme of action but not inaction. Passivity and nonviolence do not go together. Passiveness is a sign of cowardice. Our faith in something must be reflected in our action. Hence for Gandhi nonviolence can alone be practised by the strong but not by the weak.

Since nonviolence is the positive action derived from rationality there is no question of victory or defeat for a nonviolent person. All men act in the same way when they are guided by reason. Of course, when there is a conflict between two groups apparently one group wins over the other. To conquer the opponent by means of violence brings humiliation to the opponent resulting in vengeance or retaliation, but winning one's opponent through nonviolent means does not humiliate the person who is defeated. Hence one who conquers his/her opponent does not feel victory or defeat. The act of nonviolence only raises the moral standards of the individuals who practised it. At the same time they cannot feel morally superior to others. Victory and defeat arise only when there is an opposition between two individuals or groups. The aim of nonviolence is to eliminate this opposition.

Gandhi as a pragmatist realized that there are possibilities of opposition among men. Otherwise there is no differentiation in the world. But we experience differences among men on different matters. The best way to eliminate these differences is to adhere to nonviolence. Nonviolence removes the element of humiliation from the defeat. In other words, it preserves the self-respect of both the agent and the object of action. When we convince our opponent to tread the same path which we follow is to appeal to a person's reason. Thus our attitudes become identical paving the way for consensus. Thus, Gandhi maintained that there in neither compulsion nor humiliation, nor victory nor defeat when one resorts to nonviolence. According to Gandhi, at times we need to experience suffering in order to convince the opponent to see our view. In ordinary human action we make the opponent suffer but nonviolence brings suffering to its practitioners. The best way to change the heart of one's opponent is through self-suffering. Perhaps, Gandhi inadvertently brought in the example of the Christ. But there is an apparent weakness in Gandhi's argument. When we are going to convince our opponent through rational means, the question of suffering does not arise. Here the identity of purpose and opinion is established through rational considerations but not through any irrational argument or emotions. Therefore, there is no question of suffering on either side.

Of course, one must know the difference between threatening someone and imposing suffering on oneself. Any violation of a law would invite punishment. This belongs to state's purview. Gandhi substituted it through his nonviolence. Anyone's appeal to the other would be successful provided when one's suffering affects the other against whom the action is launched. Fast as a political weapon is used to protest against the authorities by many people. But it will have its impact only when the people against whom it is launched are moved by it. If people against whom one launches his fast unto death are cold then there is no result. Indifference and arrogance of the other often derail our efforts. But Gandhi's fasts were successful for the entire nation joined him to express their protests. More than the physical suffering it is the mental suffering that an individual experiences matters a lot. There is no other go if you have to convince your opponent. Gandhi's protests had their impact on people in two different ways. Since people of India reposed their absolute trust on Gandhi they suffered wherever Gandhi suffered. At the same time there was a sense of fear in the British that his fast would lead to an untoward development. The society would not spare those who were held responsible for such a despicable act. Although one has his/her own reservations regarding the fast as a political weapon, there is certainly a positive mark in it in the sense that it is more civilized to suffer oneself than allowing others to suffer.

Nonviolence has become an important value for Gandhi in his personal life. But what is surprising is that in the course of his life he realized that to live means to use violence in some form or other. Law of life is founded on the fact of death. As Martin Heidegger held all of us suffer from the anxiety of death. Gandhi initially felt that any deviation from the ideal of nonviolence would be absolutely wrong, but gradually realized that absolute nonviolence does not work in human society. Although it is not possible to be an absolute practitioner of nonviolence at least once adherence to nonviolence in principle has greater human value. The transference of nonviolence from action to its motive was exhibited in some of the critical decisions taken by Gandhi. He used to cite an example of a surgeon who performs operation as a votary of nonviolence. From the point of view of act he is inflicting pain on the patient who undergoes surgery but the surgeon's aim is to alleviate the greater suffering of the patient. Thus surgeon's motive makes his action nonviolent. We are also aware of the story of killing a calf in Gandhi's *āśrama* by administering euthanasia. The purpose here is to relieve the calf from terminal suffering. The influence of Jainism on Gandhi was very strong. Killing in any form is forbidden by Jainism. But the radical interpretation given by Gandhi to the doctrine of nonviolence is something remarkable.

Another interesting thing that we have to notice is that Gandhi always advised his followers to take to violence instead of hiding in cowardice when it comes to the question of opposing any evil. Here to be nonviolent is to oppose evil violently. Thus cowardice and nonviolence do not go together. When communal riots occurred Gandhi suggested that only a violent action can prevent such an evil. Similar logic he extended to India's action in Kashmir. When Indian army plunged into action its sole aim was to establish peace in accordance with the principle of nonviolence. It is also the case that Gandhi while working on his philosophy of nonviolence took both Jainism and the *Gītā* into consideration. There is an element of passivity in accepting suffering. At the same time following the philosophy of action of *Gītā* this passivity is discarded when it comes to opposing the evil. The transition from passivity to activity is propelled by righteous indignation in human conduct. So long as moral or righteous indignation is a mere feeling, it is passive. But this feeling transforms itself into an activity resulting in a dangerous action filled with emotion, hatred and aversion. But Gandhi opposed hatred in any form. According to him, our fight for justice is a fight against the evil but not against the actor. Thus he made a watertight distinction between a wrong and wrongdoer. What is wrong must be opposed with our might but try to reform the wrongdoer through persuasion. Thus Gandhi subscribed to the reformatory theory of punishment. Self-inflicted punishment is one of the forms of persuasion for Gandhi. But it has its own compulsion on the part of pursuer which Gandhi did not think of.

There is another important thing to be noticed in Gandhi's philosophy of action. To my mind it appears that he often ignored the distinction between violence and force. Violence is a negative force, but nonviolence is a positive force. A negative or brute force is always used for destructive purposes whereas positive force is used for constructive ones. It is the latter that dominates Gandhi's philosophy of action. Gandhi encouraged politics based on human values. He expected certain amount of code of conduct from every individual and community. Such a conduct would benefit both the individual and the community. Adherence to code of conduct is achieved through self-discipline. The progress and survival of human societies is dependent upon the disciplined individuals. Therefore a political individual must be an individual with basic human values. A civilized society is an outcome of an organized force under the control of reason. An organized force is a positive force in the sense that it protects the common interests of people. This is the first step towards the establishment of any civil society. A civil society by extending equal opportunities to all its members extends freedom, justice and happiness to them.

In fact, progressive growth of any society and Gandhi's principle of nonviolence, in a way, are interdependent. Violence destroys social harmony thus curbs the positive growth of any society. As Gandhi held Truth is the function of reason and reason opposes violence. A good social contract always uses persuasion as its method but not compulsion. The ideal rule of law based on nonviolence in a community must be extended to all communities in order to promote social justice. Thus political action and nonviolence must go hand in hand to promote peace and social harmony in any civil society. Fortunately Gandhi did not live to experience the horrors of nuclear age. The possession of weapons of mass destruction by some nations is viewed as a sign of supremacy of one nation over the other. The modern science is no more an embodiment of human dignity. Science long ago lost its value-neutral status. Mighty and wealthy alone can control science to show their dominance over the rest of the species. Science has brought us to a stage where the alternatives are pursued or perished. If reason is completely run down by might and sheer arrogance then the inevitable consequence is the disaster.

Gandhi, taking a cue from the *Gītā,* applied the principle of persuasion in his day-to-day life. Then he extended this principle to the level of society and to nations. Persuasion is the first step for any conflict resolution. It is one of the weapons which is capable of bringing down the intensity of violence. Gandhi's insistence on nonviolence had its impact on the conduct and the behaviour of the people of India. He envisaged that everyone is capable of nurturing this value of nonviolence not only to his own benefit but also for the benefit of entire society. It is not a utopian ideal. Any civil society welcomes such an ideal which makes a state of nature a state of peace and social harmony. No one wants Hobbesian state of nature where there is a war of all against all. We need our civil laws to be protected. The mechanism that regulates our civil laws must not lie outside us rather it must reside in each one of us. Certainly we need an external agency to regulate the laws of our civil society but this agency cannot exist independent of our collective will.

Nonviolence and rationality must go hand in hand. Otherwise community at large is bound to suffer. Ideologies do not matter, but in order to have peaceful coexistence with fellow citizens of society one must practise social ethics. This becomes very vital in the contemporary societies for we have people with different social and religious backgrounds. Therefore, the sense of toleration and art of persuasion become handy for settling any dispute or disagreement between two parties. People of India owe a lot to Gandhi for he inculcated these two senses in their minds. Nonviolence is not a narrow concept but is very wide to cover every aspect of human life. Our thoughts guide our actions and our language represents our thoughts. Therefore, Gandhi is right when he said nonviolence is not only applied to our actions alone but also to our thought and language. Encouraging nonviolence in any form amounts to violence. Inflicting or causing, either directly or indirectly, violence to any individual or social group is against the law of natural justice. As the French existentialist Jean-Paul Sartre held, "Man is condemned to be free". Right to life is a natural right.

Right livelihood presupposes social and economic equality. No one is deprived of one's own rights that constitute his/her freedom. Inequalities of all sorts lead to exploitation. Exploitation of any sort is also a form of violence. Gandhi was aware that it is not possible to eradicate violence completely in human societies, but must strive to reduce it to minimal level. The most dangerous of all forms of exploitation which Gandhi realized were political, social and economic. Every peace-loving individual must contribute his/her share in reducing these forms of exploitation to make a society a *Rāma-Rājya*.

Of course, people all over the world welcomed such an advice from Gandhi. But people expressed their apprehensions about Gandhi's views on science and technology. Some of his devoted followers went to extent of saying that nonviolence does not go well with industrially advanced societies. It is the machine which dominates the will of the individuals. Increase in exploitation is often linked up with the advance in civilizations which is explained in terms of technological advancement. Can man dispense with science and technology? The answer to this question is always negative. We cannot turn the wheels of times back for we do not want to live under primitive conditions. But often Gandhi is misunderstood about his views on science and technology. He never opposed science and technology, but only emphasized that there must be proper balance between scientific and moral forms of rationality in order to prevent misuse of scientific knowledge for exploitative purposes. This is echoed by the critical theorists of the Frankfurt school. There must be proper balance between scientific and moral forms of rationality. Scientific realism and philosophical idealism must go in tandem for a balanced development of any welfare society.

It is a mistake to think that nonviolence and technology do not go together. Henryk Skolimowski in his *Dancing Shiva in the Ecological Age* held that science and technology of late have become the controllers of humankind. They are no more the embodiments of human dignity. Gandhi expressed similar concerns about science and technology. Proper use of technological apparatus helps us in containing violence. Unless the necessities of human life are taken care of struggle for their possession becomes inescapable. Insecurity caused by the lack of day-to-day necessities made men fight for a larger share than required. Such a situation can be avoided only when there is adequate availability of survival needs. The reason why Gandhi disliked factory civilization was that it resulted in slums and inhuman living conditions. Thus one finds similarities between Gandhi and Marx when they opposed capitalism which is responsible for creating inhuman living conditions. Unless the congenial living conditions are restored the life of individuals would be miserable. Both Gandhi and Marx opposed inhuman conditions existing in the factories. Industrialization is good for the material progress of the nation, but it should not be promoted at the cost of congenial living conditions. Of course, modern industry is not all that barbaric. It attempts to restore human relations. It would be foolish on our part not to use science and technology for the economic growth of the nations. For the first time in human history humans started enjoying a comfortable life. What a richest man could not afford in the past is enjoyed by an ordinary citizen today. Science and technology liberated man from drudgery. We must admit this fact. It is not the fault of the science and technology if there is a wide gap between rich and poor. But it is the people who control science and technology. They created a gulf between rich and poor. We need to change their mentality through persuasion.

Inequalities have to be abolished in order to make men proud of their existence. What is lacking in one person is found in another. Therefore, everyone is endowed with certain inherent talents. Recognition of each individual's talent(s) would bring about a social change. Rationality and persuasion for Gandhi are the best tools for any social transformation. The adage "charity starts at home" holds good for everyone of us, for we need to reform ourselves first before attempting to reform others. An individual must educate himself/herself to be a member of a civilized society. We are not born as extraordinary people. There is no substitute for self-reformation. A common man does not remain common when due respect is accorded to him. By transforming little things we can transform something big. As an apostle of peace and social harmony Gandhi remained in the hearts of every peace-loving individual. He was born as an Indian and died as an Indian, but his cherished ideals transcended the boundaries of Indian subcontinent.

The present work contains seven chapters. Chapters 2-6 are exclusively devoted to a specific theme written from the perspective of Gandhi. One comes across a corpus of writings on Gandhi. But it should not be a pretext not to undertake a relook at Gandhi and his relevance to the contemporary society.

2

Peace as an Embodiment of Spirituality

GANDHI always treated peace as an embodiment of spirituality, for peace and spirituality presuppose each other. One is not in peace without being spiritual, and one cannot claim to be spiritual without being in peace. What is spirituality? How is it different from religiosity? Does one presuppose the other? These questions have to be answered before we deal with our present project. Spirituality of one kind or the other continued to exist in all human societies, and it has had tremendous impact on the lives of many great people who practised it. Spirituality is something universal and ubiquitous. It is beyond cultural, geographical, and religious limitations. Often the expressions "religion" and "spirituality" are used as synonyms. Such identification underscores the distinction between the two. This is a blasphemy committed by those who identify religion, especially any creed of religion, with spirituality. Basically the former is a doctrinaire and denominational. Religion survives as a social institution affecting the behavioural patterns of individuals living in a society. On the contrary, spirituality is not limited to any religious practice. It may be viewed that all religions promote spirituality. In fact, the manifest forms of religious worship and participation in the various religious practices must be disassociated from spirituality. It is more or less a fashion to be rational and scientific. Of course, no one denies the importance of rationality and scientific outlook in our day-to-day life, but our efforts to reduce everything to reason and scientific outlook become an unwarranted obsession for scientism. Consequently, spirituality is often treated as something highly irrational, therefore antithetical to science. This state of affairs is something alien to the Indian tradition. Of course, it is also wrong on our part to arrive at this hasty generalization, for there were a great many spiritualists in the West like Pascal, St. Francis of Assisi, St. John of the Cross, Meister Eckhart, Jacob Behme, John Bunyan and a host of others.[1]

According to the Indian tradition, science and spirituality are the two sides of the same coin. Natural and supernatural are inseparable from each other. This is evident from our day-to-day life. Spirituality is guided by a belief in what may be called the transcendent aspect of Being. In this chapter an attempt is made how Gandhi fuses peace with spirituality. According to Gandhi, to be at peace is to be spiritual. Violence of any kind is regarded as anti-spiritual.

Peace as a Form of Spirituality

Violence and peace are antithetical to each other. Each term derives its meaning from its opposite term. In a way, peace presupposes some sort of violence. It is often the case that peace is explained in terms of quietness, blissfulness, tranquillity and friendliness. Kauṭilya wrote in his *Arthaśāstra*, "peace is that which allows the enjoyment of results achieved without disturbance."[2] He believed that peace and activity are two important aspects of social progress. Similarly, the term *śānti* in the Indian context not only means peace, but also signifies quietness of mind, serenity and inner peace.

---

1 Murty 1965: 6.

2 Subramanyam 1990: 176.

The present-day world is witnessing all sorts of hostilities or civil disorders of various kinds. There is no respect for human life. Some men are treated as a means to achieve the ends of some other men. The life of some individuals is considered to be more important and precious than others. By nature, all human beings belong to the same cluster called humankind. Also, it is true that all of us are the inhabitants of the same planet Earth. But men are divided on the basis of race, caste, creed, religion, region, language and so on. These are only the accidental or external characteristics of the humans. These accidental features divide humans into the various social groups and each social group has its own culture. Each social group tries to exercise its might on the other group(s). Thus hostilities among men erupt due to their social group affinity. It is unfortunate that humans often fail to realize and recognize the fact that the essential nature of all human beings is same everywhere. This is why our grand Upaniṣadic tradition exhorted to man to know thy self first. The dictum "know thy self" is very vital and important in understanding the inner nature of man. The external dissimilarities among men are the projections of our ignorance (*avidyā*). Once we realize this fact men start treating other men as their equals. Unfortunately, what is external has become our guiding spirit in our day-to-day life. In fact, as humans, we need to introspect into our internal nature in order to find the true spirit of human life. One who realizes his/her inner nature alone can realize the meaning and purpose of human life. This does not mean that we have to ignore what is external or phenomenal completely. The phenomenal provides us with the order and configuration of external reality, which cannot be ignored. All our knowledge of incidental sciences is restricted to this phenomenal reality. Behind this external or phenomenal reality there is something inner or noumenal. The science of spirit belongs to this realm.

The great spiritual leaders, social reformers and philosophers of our country always warned us not to get influenced by the mere external features of any phenomenon, since appearances are often deceptive. These are the booby traps laid by certain selfish men. It has become the order of the day to pit one individual against another or one group against another. The result is destruction of peace and social harmony. The British conquered and ruled India for about 200 long years. The strategy adopted by them to perpetuate their sovereignty on the Indian soil is the divide and rule policy. This strategy worked out well for the British. But people cannot be fooled all the times. Sooner the people of India realized that the British were using them as a means to safeguard their vested interests. Under these circumstances the father of our nation, Gandhi, appealed to all citizens of our country to shed hatred and join together to fight for the liberation of our country from the clutches of the British. Shedding hatred is a spiritual activity. According to the *Gītā*, spirituality consists of

> fearlessness, purity, steadfastness in knowledge and concentration, charity, self-restraint, worship, study of one's scriptures, austerity, uprightness, non-violence, truth, absence of anger, renunciation, serenity, absence of calumny, compassion, non-covetousness, gentleness, modesty, absence of fickleness, energy, forgiveness, fortitude, absence of hatred and absence of pride.[3]

In fact, Gandhi's fight against the British is a nonviolent one.

Under the British rule people were not happy. They faced humiliation in the hands of the British. Often the British suppressed the unity of people. The people of India became frustrated and disheartened by the frequent British attacks on the freedom fighters. It is Gandhi who infused hope and courage into the nationalists. This resulted in the frequent launching of anti-British movements of different sorts.

[3] *Bhagavad-Gītā*, XVI.1-3.

Gandhi's role as a social reformer is something unique. He never advised his countrymen to attack the British in a violent manner. Nonviolence is his weapon. Such an approach to freedom and peace is something unique in the history of mankind.

Nonviolence as a Means to Peace

If violence is the rule rather than an exception for the British, nonviolence is the rule rather an exception for Gandhi and his followers. Gandhi's spiritualism is the outcome of his belief in the teachings of the various religions. He believes that there is no religion which does not preach the spiritual ideals such as nonviolence, compassion and love. These three spiritual ideals form the base for Gandhian philosophy. Although he remained a Hindu, Gandhi had great reverence for all religions as he believed that all the religions teach the same truth. The virtues such as nonviolence, compassion and love must be cultivated by every individual in one's social life. The cultivation of these virtues by the individuals will promote communal, social and national harmony. Like Socrates, Gandhi believed in the call of the inner voice. The actions performed by the individuals as moral agents must be in accordance with the above-mentioned virtues. Gandhi's conviction as regards these virtues is very strong

> that he even threatened that he would isolate himself from his party and retire to the forest if members did not follow him, thereby assuming all other methods involving violence and hatred were wrong.[4]

Gandhi was so convinced that he can even tame the most violent person by approaching him with nonviolence, compassion and love. According to Radhakrishnan:

---

[4] Raju: 1985: 547.

> Gandhi was first in human history to extend the principle of nonviolence from the individual to the social and political plane. He entered politics for the purpose of experimenting with nonviolence and establishing its validity.[5]

It may sound ironical that Gandhi wanted to meet Hitler and his army, if Hitler invaded our country, with an army of nonviolent, compassionate and loving souls. To quote Gandhi in this context, nonviolence is

> a force mightier than the force of arms however powerful. . . . The power that armaments give to defend right is nothing compared to the power that nonviolence gives to do the same thing and that too with better show of reason.[6]

The reason why Gandhi opted for nonviolence is that he is convinced that man is essentially good. The goodness, according to Gandhi, is the truth in man. Such goodness always prevails over evil. Gandhi appealed to people to cultivate nonviolent methods to attain the desired ends. Every individual must cultivate these virtues by means of self-discipline. A nonviolent person is not a coward rather to be nonviolent is as courageous act. It requires a highest kind of self-rule. Thus, one can be successful in one's own life provided he has the control over his own actions. A welfare society, claimed Gandhi, is one that governed by the self-controlled citizens. Such a society is an embodiment of peace and harmony.

The Spiritual Element in Satyāgraha

Gandhian philosophy is generally branded as the philosophy of *satyāgraha*. The word *satyāgraha* is often misinterpreted as "passive resistance", "nonviolence", "civil disobedience", and so on. But these interpretations of the expression *satyāgraha*

---

[5] S. Radhakrishnan 1958: XIV.

[6] M.K. Gandhi, *Hiarijan*, 14 October 1939, p. 234.

are mere results or aspects or corollaries of what Gandhi meant. As a matter of fact, such interpretations take away the inherent spiritual element involved in it. As Gandhi puts it, *satyāgraha* is nothing but passionate adherence to truth. One cannot adhere to truth unless one is a spiritual being. This is the reason why he equated Truth with God. He believed that Truth is the best qualification of God. Not only that, Truth being the law of the Universe is its support (*dharma*), everyone must follow it under all circumstances. This is what Gandhi meant by *satyāgraha.*

Truth is love, believed Gandhi. Compassion and nonviolence are the two aspects of love. He clearly stated that nonviolence without love is only a body without life. Similarly, love without nonviolence is only a disembodied spirit. In other words, nonviolence is a minimum expression of love. In this sense, *satyāgraha* is a passionate adherence to love and nonviolence. It is true that *satyāgraha* is interpreted as civil disobedience. This is due to the fact that Gandhi advised his countrymen to resist and disobey those laws imposed on them unjustly. At the same time he appealed to all those who were jailed for taking part in the civil disobedience movement to obey the rules and regulations of the jail. A *satyāgrahī* is nonviolent, but his resistance against an unjust civil law is not truly passive. It is resistance against evil. Gandhi was fully convinced with the view that if an individual is a true *satyāgrahī,* the opponent is bound to yield since love is unconquerable. In other words, love and truth do not admit of defeat. In this context one can raise a question, whether one should punish a wrongdoer? Gandhi's answer to this question is negative. God being perfect he alone can punish the wrongdoers. We being finite individuals cannot punch any other finite being since everyone of us lack perfection in one way or other. Thus Gandhi has utmost faith in God. His God is none other than Truth.

It is a known fact that the ideals of Gandhi cannot be translated into concrete realities easily, especially in social, political and international realms. Perhaps, Gandhi himself was aware of these difficulties and limitations of the application of his ideals. At the end of the British rule Gandhi confessed that his ideals can be practised by the individuals in their own capacity. When asked by some Hindus, what should they do when some Muslim rioters tried to outrage the modesty of their womenfolk? Gandhi replied that it is the duty (*dharma*) of such Hindus to protect the honour of their women even with a sword. Such an advice appears to be paradoxical. But Gandhi justified his position by stating that these Hindus are doing their duty not in hatred of the Muslims.

Summary

No one will question the legitimacy and the sublimity of Gandhian philosophy of action. He practised everything that he preached. He converted his ideals into concrete realities. Thus there is a link between his theory and practice. But the present-day society may not imbibe the ideals of Gandhi, since it finds it difficult to accommodate them. At the best we can say that Gandhian ideals work only if both the parties in dispute are earnest about each other's welfare. In other words, each group must realize the sanctity of human life. Such realization is possible only when people realize that the essential nature of every individual is the same, and the differences are only artificial.

Although Gandhian philosophy is not bereft of any world-view, Gandhi never worked out a systematic philosophy. He was too much involved in his action to work out all the implications of what he believed. The spiritual element in Gandhian philosophy is reflected in his life and action. One does not find any systematic epistemology or ontology in Gandhian philosophy. His view of life always transcended the limits of ordinary experiences. Like early Ludwig

Wittgenstein, perhaps, Gandhi might have thought that values exist outside this ordinary world of experience. But these values of Gandhi are not merely conditioned by formal principles of logic but they have logic of their own. The spiritual way of life is a form of life. Its grammar is conditioned by intuition and insight. The spiritual form of life, unlike ordinary life experiences, needs special effort from the individual(s) to segregate it from ordinary mundane experiences. It is empathy rather than sympathy that dominates the spiritualism of Gandhi. Being pragmatic in his attitude Gandhi never tried to construct a set of theories to resolve human problems. One finds an element of spiritualism in his mental make up.

Simplicity has been an important element of spiritualism. Gandhi's quest for simplicity is seen in his attitude towards the religions of the world. The simple truth of our life is to realize that God is nothing but truth. Therefore, simplicity in thought, action and attitude make one a spiritual being. Also, one can notice that Gandhi is not an extraordinary human being. One can say that he is an ordinary human being with an extraordinary yearning for excellence and extraordinary capacity to achieve what he wanted. Therefore one can see extraordinary person in an ordinary human being. Transparency is another characteristic feature of a spiritual person. One could see transparency in his thought, act and living. Like any other ordinary man Gandhi too committed Himalayan blunders. What is characteristic of Gandhi is that he never asked anyone to do that very thing which he could not do by himself. There lies the greatness of Gandhi.

Gandhi held that there is inherent capacity in everyone of us to respond to noble impulses. But often we fail to respond because we do not allow our conscience to act freely.

3

Conflict Resolution

No one leads a life without experiencing conflicts of one sort or the other in so far as he/she is a member of a society. A society is a dynamic organic whole wherein people enter into a diversity of social relationships with each other. In the absence of such relationships, the life of an individual becomes miserable. At the same time, these are the relationships which often lead to conflicts of different sorts both at individual and social levels. As a matter of fact, conflict is a part of any healthy relation. Agreements and disagreements between individuals and social groups is a common phenomenon. Instead of trying to avoid a conflict, it is better to learn how to resolve a conflict. The mismanagement of any conflict results in an unhealthy relationship. On the contrary, when a conflict is resolved in a positive way it helps people to understand each other more closely than ever. Personal, professional and social relationships become stronger and healthier when conflicts arising out of them are handled skilfully.

Conflicts cannot be treated as isolated incidents that can be resolved or managed offhandedly, but are part and parcel of society's ongoing evolution and development. Conflicts are not always negative or destructive occurrences, but are also positive productive forces that contribute to the growth of a society. Conflict transformation is not merely an approach or a set of techniques, but a way of thinking about and understanding the root cause of a conflict. Conflict transformation is a process that is non-violent for it tries to deal with conflicts that are deep-rooted and constantly perpetuate violence. An attempt is made in this chapter to address the problem in question from the perspective of Gandhi.

Genesis of a Conflict

We encounter conflicts of different nature both at individual and social level. If a conflict is taken in its positive sense then it establishes a healthy relationship among individuals. The mentality of two people cannot be the same, but can be similar. It is not necessary that we agree with each other on all points all the time. What is important in one's life is to face the conflict rather than avoiding it, for its avoidance may lead to further complications. At the same time, the mismanagement of a conflict leads to unhealthy consequences. Thus conflict resolution occupies an important place both in the personal and social life of the individuals. The question is how to resolve a conflict? What are the ways in which a conflict can be handled in order to establish a healthy relationship between the parties involved in the conflict? There are different approaches to conflict resolution.

Conflicts arise out of differences, and these differences are due to the disagreement over values, motivations, perceptions, ideas and desires. At times these differences may appear to be trivial, but they trigger strong feelings, and a deep personal need may be there at the bottom of the problem. One has to recognize the needs of the both the parties in conflict in order to build a long-time relationship. This is to say that one cannot ignore the needs of both the parties involved in the conflict. Maintaining personal relationships is an important factor in the social life of the individuals. Often these relationships collapse due to misunderstanding between two parties. These misunderstandings arise for each one fails to recognize the needs of the other. We often become self-centred. Such an attitude towards the other results in maintaining distance, arguments and finally our relationships end-up in break-ups. The conflicts in workplace are very common for they arise out of the professional rivalry between two parties. One has to examine the legitimacy of these conflicts. Soul searching is absolutely necessary on the part of each individual to build up healthy working relationships. In the absence of such healthy relationships among the individuals both the individuals and the organization(s) are bound to suffer.

One has to realize that a conflict is not merely a disagreement between two parties. It is a situation in which both the parties anticipate threat to each other. Conflicts become more and more problematic if they are not nipped in the bud. We have to respond to the conflicts based on our perceptions of our own life experiences, culture, beliefs and values. There is a danger if we do not control our emotions in times of stress. These emotions perpetuate conflicts of sorts and we do not find any solution outside us for the problem is within us. The positive aspect of conflicts is that they aid us in terms of personal and societal growth when we are able to resolve them amicably. In fact, they serve as trust builders. We come to know that our relationship with other is secure when it can withstand challenges and opposition.

Sometimes conflicts may be more threatening than they really are when our perceptions of a conflict arise from our nightmares of the past. A sense of pessimism springs from our past experiences which drive us to the belief that all our present-day disagreements would end up in unwanted results. Thus we see conflicts in relationships as demoralizing, dangerous and frustrating. There is a need to come out of these early childhood traumatizing experiences in order to resolve conflicts. However, if one thinks that every conflict is a dangerous one then it is nothing but an imagination of that individual. One should not attempt to approach any conflict with a negative or closed mind. If one does it then there is a chance of one becoming more and more aggressive or a complete introvert. The aggressive nature turns one into a violent person and the introvert shuts down without any response.

Normally psychologists advocate a stress management therapy for a successful conflict resolution at the individual level. One of the things expected from an individual to resolve a conflict is to possess the capacity to recognize and respond to the things that matter to the other. One's reactions must be calm, non-defensive, and respectful. One must be in a position to forget and forgive in order to move ahead the conflict by overcoming resentment and anger. Also, one must develop the ability to arrive at compromise by avoiding punishing. It is always better to face a conflict directly with the party involved in the conflict. But conflict resolution at the social level requires a collective consciousness to resolve the conflict amicably.

Social Conflicts

Conflicts at social level may cause damage to the very progress of a society or a state or a nation. Nation building involves a collective effort on the part of its citizens. As a pacifist Gandhi's sole weapon is nonviolence. It is the only meaningful and sane tactic or strategy in the social struggle.[1] Truth and nonviolence always go together for Gandhi. There is no other way of resolving a conflict excepting the way of truth. To quote Ethel Manin in this context:

> To give back violence for violence is to sink to the level of a tyrant, who understands power only in terms of death and

1 Manin 2006: 177.

> destruction; the power of non-violent methods of resistance is the power of life, of the unquenchable spirit.[2]

Peace prevails only when there is an environment which is filled with truth. Animosity, fear, anger and cowardice are the root causes of any conflict. One cannot expect peace in such an environment. Of course, every individual must possess the capability to resolve conflicts at the individual level before tackling the conflicts at the social level.

For Gandhi, truth and God are one and the same. There are two kinds of truth, namely, absolute and relative. Given the imperfect nature of man, it is not all that easy to realize the absolute truth.[3] On the contrary relative truth refers to the immediate goals of individuals in their day-to-day life which are realizable. Does one see any conflict between absolute and relative forms of truth? There is none. The absolute truth serves as a regulative principle (*dharma*) to guide us in pursuing our day-to-day relative truths. One can reach the highest or absolute truth through relative truth. Gandhi firmly believed that God's existence and the essence of human unity are all-pervasive. Therefore, there is no human being who does not realize this truth. Gandhi was successful in realizing this truth in his day-to-day encounters.[4]

The only way, according to Gandhi, to discover truth is to adhere to nonviolence. Human life is always beset with conflicts of different types. We have already discussed this matter. Nuclear warfare did make us realize that war is not the remedy for any conflict resolution. Even the emperor Aśoka realized his blunder after the great Kaliṅga war. For whose sake did he fight the war? Did he bring happiness to his own

---

2 Manin 2006: 178.

3 Only a perfect mind alone can grasp what is absolute. It is the mind's inner eye that grasps this absolute.

4 Gregg 1960: 168.

people by winning the war? War can never settle the conflicts. War is the result of collective anger. It is here in this context we need to examine the role of nonviolence in avoiding war which is destructive of peace and social harmony.[5]

Is nonviolence a kind of resistance? How can anyone practise nonviolence as a method of resistance in the contemporary world? Any resistance must be backed by great strength, power and weapons in order to be successful. But there were incidents in the past that show great courage, deep conviction and a genuine cause always turned victorious without any violence. Our own freedom struggle against the mighty British forces is one such incident. Gandhi believed that love and the desire for justice lead us to unity. Unity is the best remedy for conflict resolution. Peace and truth coexist for Gandhi. Lying is dangerous for it leads to conflicts and violence when it is exposed. A truthful man cannot be violent for he realizes that there is no need to be violent in achieving what is desirable. There is no shortcut to truth. We must keep nonviolence as the goal in order to achieve freedom. The attainment of freedom is in exact proportion to the attainment of nonviolence.[6]

How to Practise Nonviolence?

Gandhi remained a pragmatist throughout his life. He never preached anything to his followers unless he practised it. By practising nonviolence, Gandhi claimed to have resolved conflicts of various types. Fraud, deceit, conceit, lying, violence and untruth have no room for Gandhi in his personal life.[7] The secret of his success he wants to share with everyone who volunteers to adhere to it. There is no secret for truth.

---

[5] Gregg 1960, preface.

[6] M.K. Gandhi, *Young India*, 20 May 1926.

[7] Ibid., 31 December 1931.

Truth is an open book. The more open one is the more truthful he/she is. An individual who follows truth and non-violence never faces any defeat in his life. He hardly faces despair. When truth and nonviolence go together there is no weapon which can stop their success. Weapons can only destroy precious human life but cannot establish truth.

Gandhi held that nonviolence works like a mathematical operation. The triangle that a mathematician draws is not a particular triangle but it is the essence of all triangles. Similarly, the real world is not visible to our ordinary eye but has to be experienced with the inner eye. Gandhi did not turn a blind eye to scientific temper. According to him, all living forces require suitable stimuli to react or respond. In the absence of such stimuli there is no growth. These stimuli may come from different sources. But all our reactions or responses must be properly guarded by the principle of nonviolence. At no point of time violence should be part of our response or reaction to our stimuli. But the question arises: does the exercise of nonviolence have any limits? According to Gandhi, to exercise nonviolence requires more courage than fighting with a sword. Cowardice and nonviolence do not go together. Nonviolence is a virtue and a virtue is always consistent. It is a conscious and deliberate act. It is more an individual's conviction rather than an external imposition.[8]

Nonviolence springs from the eternal law of love. There is no other tool which can successfully work to resolve any conflict. Jesus preached us the eternal law of love for otherwise his life would not have attracted the attention of anyone.[9] Nonviolence is not merely a personal virtue but also a social virtue to be cultivated by all of us as humans. A society cannot sustain without nonviolence. Nonviolence regulates social

---

[8] M.K. Gandhi, *Young India*, 12 August 1926.

[9] M.K. Gandhi, *Harijan*, 17 January 1939.

disharmony. Therefore, it is extended to national and international scale to promote universal peace.

The practice of nonviolence does not mean that one does not interfere in the affairs of others. When there is a need one has to interfere in stopping a violent fight between two individuals risking one's own life. Thus nonviolence makes an individual a courageous person. According to Gandhi, right means lead to right ends. Violence can lead to further violence. Violence as a means to unavoidable self-defence perpetuated wars in the history of mankind. This unending violence in the form of wars led to mad race of armaments and unwanted weapons. Maintaining the arsenal becomes the priority of nations rather than looking after the welfare of citizens. The violence of the aggressor can defeat the superior violence of the defender.[10] Violence can never mitigate violence. It is like a wildfire. The only way to put an end to violence is to adhere to nonviolence. Gandhi in his personal life experienced this cardinal truth.[11]

Compromise and trust are the two constitutive aspects of nonviolence, according to Gandhi. Even when one is cheated by his opponent more than once still one should not lose trust in him, for implicit trust in human nature is the essence of this creed. Similarly, compromise teaches us to adjust to realities in order to avoid conflicts even at the cost of one's own position. If we do not employ compromise and trust in conflict resolution then no conflict would be settled.

Power of Nonviolence

There have been successful attempts of use of nonviolence in different nations at different times. Richard B. Gregg, the American social philosopher, analysed the significance of non-

---

10 Ibid., 1 September 1940.

11 Ibid., 30 March 1947.

violence in his interesting work *The Power of Non-Violence* published in 1934. Politics and wars preoccupy the writings of historians in general. They pay hardly any attention to other significant events in the history of mankind. There were incidents in the past where nonviolence was taken up by individuals, en masse in a corporate form. Nonviolence by a mass is more significant than anything else. Gregg cites a number of examples. Some of them are as follows: Champaran Movement in India (1917); Kotgarh Movement in Shimla (1921); Vykom *satyāgraha* in the state of Travancore (1925); Bardoli Movement (1928); struggle for Indian Independence; Montgomery Movement in USA (1956); and anti-apartheid movement by Mandela in South Africa.[12] Even Albert Einstein, while appreciating the power of nonviolence, held that in the age of debunking moral system Gandhi as a statesman set an example to show humankind how to maintain higher human relations on the basis of justice and law rather than on brute power.

According to S. Radhakrishnan, Gandhi always felt that those who use force a weapon adopt the Darwinian struggle for existence. They do not distinguish the distinction between animal and human worlds and impose biological generalization into a doctrine of human destiny. Use of violence in human world degrades the level of human existence to animal existence.[13] As mentioned earlier, religious, political and economic conflicts have preoccupied our present-day life. The conflicts among the different religious faiths have become common phenomena. Even in the same religious faith there is a conflict between fundamentalists and moderates. Political conflicts often arise out of feeling of supremacy of one nation over the other, one state over the other and so on. The

---

[12] Gregg 1960: 3-39.

[13] Radhakrishnan 1977: 21.

economic conflicts are basically between developed and developing and underdeveloped nations. Conflicts can be minimized only when we recognize the needs of the other. As Michael Brecher[14] puts it, crisis, conflict and war are interrelated. They have common origin in the sense of distrust. At present the world is at the threshold of destruction. We have to decide either to have future or no future at all. If we are interested in the future of humankind then we need to spread the sense of trust and cooperation through the Gandhian methodology of truth and nonviolence. There is no other way except resorting to this Gandhian paradigm.

Gandhian paradigm always starts from those who are deprived of their basic rights or advantages. It may be the people of a nation or a nation by itself. Those who are affluent must share part of their affluence to extend the dignity of human life to those who are in dire need of it. Recognizing the need of others would be the first step in this exercise. As we are aware of the fact that poverty is the major contributor to any conflict. There are poor in every nation. The division between the rich and poor resulted in the major economic conflict in the contemporary world. Rich is becoming more and more rich, and the poor more and more poor. Thus there is a drastic economic polarization. This is one of the major conflicts in the contemporary world. According to Anurag Gangal,[15] *New International Economic Order* needs to borrow much from Gandhian paradigm to settle this major economic conflict. Gandhi suggested that nonviolent crafts are those which are fundamentally free from violence and exploitation. These crafts help people lead a dignified human life without destroying their peace. As highlighted by Kumarappa,[16] the

---

[14] Brecher 1996.

[15] Gangal 1985.

[16] Kumarappa 1951.

eleven vows of Gandhi are essential for the establishment of an ideal society. They are: truth, love, *brahmacarya*, non-possession, non-stealing, bread labour, control of the palate, fearlessness, equality of religion, untouchability and *swadeshi*. But we are living in a technological age where some of these vows cannot be practised. There is always competition between one individual and the other. But truth and love are the two most important virtues to be cultivated.

Summary

It is not all that easy to follow Gandhian paradigm of love and nonviolence for the creation of a qualitatively better society. It requires a lot of conviction and sacrifice on the part of the follower of Gandhian paradigm. At times his teachings appear to be the sermons given to the masses by the Pope from a pulpit. No one denies that Gandhi practised whatever he preached. To the extent possible people aim at cultivating these virtues (truth and nonviolence) in order to lead a life of peace and harmony. But there are limitations which make an individual aggressive and berserk. We need to probe into the social factors responsible for the aggressive and unruly behaviour of an individual(s). Mark Juergensmeyer in his interesting work *Gandhi's Way: A Handbook of Conflict Resolution* tries to show that Gandhian paradigm is the only legitimate paradigm for any conflict resolution. He writes that "Gandhi was a fighter."[17] Prima facie this statement appears to be paradoxical for it shows that one of the staunch pacifists of the contemporary times is described as a fighter. But Gandhi was a different kind of fighter, according to Juergensmeyer. It is a nonviolent fight to establish truth. Gandhi's passive non-resistance to oppression and evil incorporates certain elements of the opponent's position into one's own position. There is a vision of truth on both sides, but it is incomplete.

---

[17] Juergensmeyer 2005: ix.

The vision of truth would be complete only when a *stayāgrahī* takes into account the vision of his opponent which is partly true. All other means such as boycotts, non-cooperation, demonstrations and strikes are only meant to attract the attention of the opponent. Gandhi always discouraged people going to court of law for settlements, although he was a trained lawyer. He believed that strict adherence to law sometimes hampers the peace process. In order to satisfy both the parties involved in conflict one needs to get into the root cause of the problem. Law does not address the root of a problem. This made Gandhi to hold the view that law "seldom allow(s) for a judgement to which both sides can agree with equal satisfaction."[18] Thus law leaves scope for another conflict instead of settling the existing one. Thus it is inner voice rather than the reason that helps us in resolving a conflict. Sometimes it is true that a model that worked well in one society may not work in another social set-up although the essential nature of all human beings one and the same. Perhaps, Gandhi harps on this essential nature rather than on accidental human creations such as society. But Juergensmeyer argues that Gandhi's paradigm works like a pill to settle conflicts between families, friends, neighbours, and co-workers in all cultures. But the danger is that how does this paradigm work when the opponent hardly cares for anyone of the human values. His aim is to just win by hook or crook. Thus Juergensmeyer's argument in favour Gandhi's paradigm meets the dead end.[19]

But Juergensmeyer's analysis of Northern Ireland conflict provides a breather to Gandhian paradigm. The tentative peace process started only when the conflicting groups admitted that they committed crimes and each side had grievances

---

[18] Juergensmeyer 2005: 7.

[19] Cole 2005-06: 197-200.

against the other. And both the sides know that strict adherence to the rule of law would not settle the issue for both the sides committed atrocities. Now Gandhian paradigm has a role to play although inadvertently it undermined human rights. The solution aims at making belligerents to forget the crimes committed by them in the past. The "no-fault" principle is invoked here. The unfortunate consequence of this principle is that no one is found guilty of the crimes committed by them.

Similarly, *satyāgraha* too has its limitations. A case study provided by Juergensmeyer reveals this fact. The tragic resistance of Jews living in the Warsaw Ghetto against the Nazi regime is a testimony to this fact. Gandhi's letter to the threatened leaders advising them to challenge the Nazis openly resulted in a disaster. They were shot dead. The view that we have to stay "open to communication and self-criticism" and "regard your opponent as a potential allay"[20] does not work with an opponent with cold mind. Here is the fight between Jews and Nazis which is akin to the case of a rape. Certainly it is not open to the possibilities of *satyāgraha*. But Gandhi advised people to resort to violence, even if it is physical and coercive, to resist rape. Gandhi held that resistance is more honourable than inaction. But this advice of Gandhi does not go well with his view that violence is evil. But Juergensmeyer argues in favour of Gandhi stating that there is a difference between coercion and "detentive coercion". Rape is a form of "detentive coercion". Therefore, immediate resistance to such coercion in the form of violence is allowed for there would be no damage done to opponent. It disables the opponent without destroying him. Suppose the opponent is killed in the process then would it be treated as a violent act on the part of the defender? Reinhold Niebuhr would not see any analogy between a rape case and the

---

[20] Cole 2005-06: 63.

animosity between Jews and Nazis. The latter is not a case of detentive coercion. Therefore, Gandhian paradigm does not offer solutions to many conflicts. Hayim Greenberg in his open letter to Gandhi (1937) held that a Jewish Gandhi would have the privilege of living only for five minutes before the Gestapo agent lead him to the gallows. What we must note from this experience is that Gandhian paradigm cannot be the only paradigm to settle conflicts of types. We must also realize its limitations.

4

Corruption and Human Values

LIKE GOOD and evil, honesty and dishonesty coexist in any human society. It is the dishonesty that drives us to corrupt practices. Corruption has become part and parcel of our day-to-day life. Most of us are, knowingly or unknowingly, roped into corrupt practices. Somehow we have to live with it. This is not a new phenomenon but an age-old phenomenon. In the past people used to resort to corrupt practices to get their things done in a discrete manner. In modern societies corruption has become an open commodity. It is like a terminal disease and is going to haunt every human society as long as human race survives. A simple definition of corruption is that any deviation from normally established practice, which has legitimate social approbation, is called a corrupt practice. There are innumerable forms of corruption. It is not only for the sake of material gain a person resorts to corrupt practices, but also to prevent any social mechanism from doing good to people or community of individuals. The recent movements against corruption clearly show that corruption has gone beyond the limits. It has percolated into every form of social life. Bribery and doing favours for one's own advantages are common corrupt practices. By and large, greed and power make persons corrupt. Unless one cultivates basic human values it is difficult to contain corruption in social life. No external mechanism would ever help us to mitigate corruption. Even if it helps, it is done only at surface level. The real feeling against corruption must come from within.

This is what Gandhi advocated time and again. However, it is true that we cannot completely root out corruption, yet we must see to that honesty does not disappear from our social and personal life. All of us are concerned with corruption but we lack commitment to fight corruption. In this paper an attempt is made to examine whether human values can mitigate corrupt practices as envisaged by Gandhi.

Shades of Corruption

There are various forms of corruption. Although it is not all that easy to define what corruption is, yet all of us are capable of identifying a corrupt practice. As held by the social contract theorists like John Locke and Jean-Jacques Rousseau, man by nature is good. But he becomes corrupt when he enters into social relationships. His good nature is vitiated by greed and power. These self-centred actions of man derail expected social progress. Stealing, lying, conceit, deceit, lethargy, lack of commitment and complete dependence on others promote corruption in any civilized society. The two most important forms of corruption are private and public. In its private form, corruption destroys the life of an individual. For instance, one who indulges in gambling, adultery, smoking and drinking gradually destroys himself. His destruction is self-caused. In other words, he becomes victim of his own vices. Suppose he is the sole breadwinner of his family, along with him he is going to destroy the lives of his dependents. The public form of corruption is more dangerous in the sense that it cripples entire social governance. An individual or a group of individuals indulge in corrupt practices causing enormous loss to states' exchequer. The recent 2G Spectrum scam, mining scam, smuggling of banned substances and metals, drug pedalling, illegal manufacturing of drugs and spurious liquor, illegal arms trade, production of counterfeits of currency, leaking out strategic information to our enemies, match fixing, fudging the account of a company by the people in armed forces are a few examples for public form of corruption. The individual or the group involved in these scams ropes others into this form of corruption so that it is concealed from the public eye. Politicians, bureaucrats, businessmen, men in uniform and middlemen often assist these corrupt. In the process, a chain is created and every link of this chain is carefully guarded to carry on with their illegal activities. Sometimes whistleblowers help the state to unearth such corrupt practices. But many of them are liquidated by these mafia gangs. Some of the scams were unearthed in the past in our country and the men behind these scams were arrested and put on trail.

There were incidents where politicians were removed or asked to resign from their portfolios on graft charges. In 1990s, the then prime minister of Thailand, Silpa Archa was asked to step down on the charges of corruption. During the same period several ministers, governors and chief ministers of the various provinces in India were also asked to vacate their seats on corruption charges. Most of these people were involved in what is called *hawālā* racket. Their names were found in the diary of a businessman who bribed them for getting some favours. These dishonest practices mainly intend to achieve maximum with minimum effort. In such circumstances honesty is put on hold. Such a situation poses serious threat to democracy and dignified public life. Although we witness tremendous progress in science and technology, yet there is considerable decay in the social standards of individuals. With money politicians acquire power and with power they acquire money. This is a vicious circle. Money power and muscle power are completely destroyed the honest life of individuals. Mafias and gangsters are ruling the roost.

It is a matter of serious concern to all of us that we are witnessing unethical practices in all forms of social life of individuals. Honest politicians, bureaucrats, people in education field have become a rare breed. If this is the situation, how do we protect ourselves from these corrupt men? Should we close our eyes? Is there any remedy to minimize corruption, if not eradication? These are the questions that constantly haunt us.

The Role of Human Values

Human values form an integral part of human societies. As aptly remarked by Plato, a just society is that which is constituted by the just individuals. A just individual is one who does not allow his irrational part of the soul to dominate his rational part. If we allow our irrational part of the soul which is characterized by the spirit and appetite, then there is bound to be social disharmony. The human values are the product of the rational part of the soul. In order to maintain social progress and harmony among the citizens and the various limbs of the society we need to cultivate values. A value is something desirable. What is desired by an individual may not be desirable for others in the society. Therefore, a value has an intrinsic worth. As it is held in the Indian tradition, all of us act in accordance with the impulses born out of our own nature and our nature is conditioned by the combination of *sattva, rajas* and *tamas*. *Sattva* is responsible for intelligence and illumination, *rajas* for bravery and chivalry, and *tamas* for dullness. Every one of us possesses them in the various permutations and combinations. The temperament and the behaviour of each individual are dependent on the combination of these three *guṇa*s. This is the reason why people think, act and judge differently. All our ideological and attitudinal differences are due to these varying combinations. The positive aspect of such combinations is that each one of us is endowed with a unique capability or talent which would be put to the beneficial use of all. Such a view has resulted in the stratification of social classes. And each social class has its definite role to play in the making of a welfare or egalitarian society. This is the reason why Gandhi supported the *varṇa dharma*. His intention is not certainly to create any difference or hierarchy among these social classes. As Koller puts it:

> Essentially, a *varṇa* is a theory of social organization whereby the individuals in society are divided into different classes with different functions in society according to differing personal characteristics and different social needs. The theory is that the good of society will be furthered if there are different classes of individuals who will perform the different tasks requisite for a good life in society.[1]

In other words, the division of labour among the various social classes will benefit every individual of the society. Just as we do not say that our legs are inferior to our head, we do not say that one social class is superior to the other. If anyone does it, it goes against the very spirit of *varṇa dharma*, for *varṇa* in its primordial sense does not represent caste. *Varṇa* (social class) of an individual is decided according to his qualifications, tendencies and dispositions. On the contrary, castes are distinguished from one another not by the qualification of the individual but by heredity, dietary regulations, endogamy and exogamy, occupation and place in the pecking order. Caste is typically a modern expression which is etymologically derived from the Portuguese expression *casta*. It is typically used to classify people on the basis of their birth.[2] Human values remind every one of us of our duties as obligations. Rights and duties are the two sides of the same coin. One cannot talk of rights without performing one's duties. The duties of man as a man and the duties of man as a member of a particular social class are very much

---

1 Koller 1970: 37.

2 Ibid.: 38.

grounded in the very order of the universe. The universe is essentially moral. Everything that happens in the universe is for the benefit of the whole. Man is not an exception to this rule. He occupies a special place in the order of things in the universe. He is expected to perform his duties as obligations to maintain peace and harmony in order to promote the well-being of the universe in general. Sin and evil, which are the manifestations of the corrupt practices, perpetuate when individuals refuse to those things which benefit the society as a whole. Selfish pursuits by individuals derail social harmony and progress. A decadent moral system destroys the universe of its moral sanctity.

Although we talk of what is expected of each individual for promoting social harmony and progress, there is enough provision in the Indian tradition for every individual to realize his goals of life (*puruṣārthas*). The four important goals of life advanced by the Indian tradition are: righteousness (*dharma*), means of life (*artha*), enjoyment (*kāma*) and liberation (*mokṣa*). These goals were discussed by the great Hindu law givers, Manu and Kauṭilya. They are incorporated in the great Hindu epic, *Mahābhārata*. These goals of life are the social principles underlying the social classes and stages of life as advocated in *Gītā*. The good life is defined in terms of these goals of human life. Having admitted that man is a combination of material and spiritual elements, it is necessary to satisfy his material and spiritual needs. Before satisfying one's spiritual needs, one has to satisfy one's material needs. Therefore, *artha* and *kāma* precede *mokṣa*. *Dharma* has an important role to play in the regulation of attainment of means of life and enjoyment. Thus it is an overarching principle that regulates our material and mental life. Although the expression *dharma* has many connotations, with respect to society *dharma* provides the rules for settling disputes and conflicts that arise in the course of social life of man. If the conflicts are kept to a minimum, then the society can be well maintained. In this context, *dharma* has a social sense and significance. It is true that man does not merely live on righteousness and justice alone. He requires both *artha* and *kāma* for it is natural to any social life. One cannot expect every man to be a sage or saint. Kauṭilya writes in his *Arthaśāstra* that the substance of mankind is termed *artha*, the earth that contains mankind is *artha*.[3]

Etymologically, the word *artha* is derived from the Sanskrit root *ri* which means "that which one goes for". Thus *artha* can be interpreted as anything that is sought after. As ordinary social beings, we aspire for wealth, position, profit, property, precious things and so on. Further, both *Mahābhārata* and *Pañcatantra* reveal one's attitude towards *artha*. According to *Mahābhārata:*

> What is regarded as *dharma* here depends entirely upon wealth (*artha*). One who robs another of wealth robs him of his *dharma* as well. Poverty is a state of sinfulness. All kinds of meritorious acts flow from the possession of great wealth, as from wealth spring all religious acts, all pleasures, and heaven itself. Wealth brings about accession of wealth, as elephants capture elephants. Religious acts, pleasure, joy, courage, worth, and learning; all these proceed from wealth. From wealth one's merit increases. He that has no wealth has neither this world nor the next.[4]

Even the tradition collection of the tales of wisdom known as *Pañcatantra* highlights the advantages of wealth. To quote from it:

> The smell of wealth (*artha*) is quite enough to wake a creature's sterner stuff. Wealth gives constant rigour, confidence, and power. Poverty is a curse worse than death. Virtue without wealth is of no consequence. The lack of money is the root of all evil.[5]

---

[3] Balasubramanian 1991: 59.

[4] Koller 1970: 11.

[5] Ibid.: 10.

The above passages from *Mahābhārata* and *Pañcatantra* should not be misinterpreted and misunderstood. *Artha* as one of the goals of human life refers to all necessary means of life. What is highlighted here is the means to biological and social life. Of course, the means to spiritual life are not excluded. In other words, biological and social life is a prerequisite for spiritual life. It is *dharma* that regulates the misuse of *artha*. Therefore, no *artha* is pursued in violation of *dharma*. Mere accumulation of wealth is not an end in itself. *Artha* is only a means to enjoyment (*kāma*). *Kāma* is another important goal of life. Man seeks satisfaction, pleasure and enjoyment in his social life. In the absence of *kāma*, life becomes dry and miserable. In Vātsyāyana's *kāmasūtra*, *kāma* is defined as

> the enjoyment of the appropriate objects of five senses of hearing, feeling, seeing, tasting, and smelling, assisted by the mind, together with the soul. The ingredient in this is a peculiar contact between the organ of sense and its object, and the consciousness of pleasure that results from the contact is called *kāma*.[6]

While discussing the relationship between *dharma*, *artha* and *kāma*, Manu wrote:

> Some declare that the good of man consists in the *dharma* and *artha*; others opine that it is found in *artha* and *kāma*; some say that *dharma* alone will give it; the rest assert that *artha* alone is the chief good in the harmonious coordination of the three.[7]

It is natural for sensible human beings to look for the satisfaction of their desires for food, drink, clothing, sex and other sensual pleasures. The denial of sensual pleasures may lead to frustration and there is every chance of an individual becoming perverted. Instead, sensuous pleasures have to be

---

6 Sharma 1979: 14.

7 Ibid.: 15.

regulated. In a way, the indulgence in sensuous pleasures through material desires, an individual sets himself for the spiritual quest. According to Upaniṣads, *ātman* is the power behind the powers of universe. If this were the case then the ultimate perfection of man is possible only through self-realization. Such realization sets man free from bondage. There is no death for *ātman,* the power behind the Universe. One has to transcend one's biological and social existence to reach the spiritual heights. In fact, man has all the inbuilt potential within himself to realize the supreme self. Man has to translate his potency into actuality so that he realizes his own perfection. In other words, after satisfying the needs of his biological and social life man has to satisfy his spiritual life also.

The goals of life provide direction to humanity. They provide answer to man's fundamental question: What does man seek in life, or, how should he lead his life? As a biological and social being he is conditioned by certain desires. In fact, *dharma, artha, kāma* and *mokṣa* are normative concepts that provide an orientation to human life. Each concept is an embodiment of a rule. The function of a normative rule is to guide the behaviour of an individual in society. Unless our actions are guided by certain normative considerations, they suffer from lack of proper orientation. The ancient Indian tradition prescribed these normative principles to individuals to find meaning and purpose in their life. The pursuance of these goals of life does not lead to division of life rather it must be seen as ordering one's life and his activities. One does not see any conflict between one goal of life and the other in so far as they are regulated by the principle of *dharma.*

Gandhian Solution to Corruption

Gandhi admired the traditional Indian value system for he believed it to be the only legitimate weapon against corruption. If each individual performs his duty/duties as obligation/ obligations towards the well-being of the society in which he is a member, then most of the problems are solved. Each one of us must realize that we are the partners working for the public good. There must be complete probity on the part of the individuals. We must watch our thoughts and deeds. Introspection and remorsefulness alone can keep us on the right track.

It appears that Gandhi held that if anyone wants to join his *āśrama* must obey the ten vows prescribed by him. The most important of these ten is non-thieving (*aparigraha*). This is one of the most important vows, which is wider in scope than its usual meaning. To put it in the words of Gandhi:

> I suggest that we are thieves in a way. If I take anything that I do not need for my own immediate use and keep it, I thieve it from somebody else. I am no socialist, and I do not want to dispossess them who have got possessions; but I do not say that personally those who want to see light out of darkness have to follow this rule. I do not want to dispossess anybody, I should then be departing from the rule of nonviolence (one of the vows). In India we have got many millions of people who have to be satisfied with one meal a day. You and I have no right to anything we really have until these many millions are clothed and fed. You and I, who ought to know better, must adjust our wants, and even undergo voluntary privation, in order that they may be nursed, fed, and clothed.[8]

In an egalitarian society, Gandhi's above observations may not have any value. But a society which is polarized between poverty and affluence certainly needs to pay attention to his observations. Gandhi's views are perfectly humane in their spirit. Any poor society must not indulge in any kind of extravagance at the cost of the lives of those who are living below the poverty line. Unwanted consumption and hoarding of the essential commodities is not only a dishonest act but also a crime against the poor. Time and again Gandhi held

8 Gandhi 1933: 384-85.

that there is no other rule on corruption than "zero tolerance". His aversion to corrupt practices of any kind is conspicuous in his speeches and writings. In May 1939 he held that:

> I would go to the length of giving the whole congress a decent burial, rather than put up with the corruption that is rampant.[9]

Gandhi always aired his views on corruption without any kind of restraint. He held that it is the duty of all those in authority to deal with the menace of corruption sternly. Any indifferent attitude towards corruption can be legitimately called a criminal offence. He was upset with those who indulged in corruption, directly or indirectly, while holding the power. Lack of vigilance and moral courage to fight corruption, according to Gandhi, is a sign of cowardice. To put it in the words of Gandhi:

> It (corruption) has now become worse than before. Restraint from it has practically gone. Corruption will go when the large number of persons given unworthily to it realize that the nation does not exist for them to exploit but that they exist to serve the nation. This requires morals, and extreme vigilance on the part of those who are free of the taint. Indifference will be criminal.[10]

Gandhi himself witnessed the tremendous growth in corruption during 1939-48. He was alarmed by its rapidity and its successful control over the human life. As a last resort to curb this insidious menace called corruption, Gandhi appealed to people to adhere to the traditional human values. According to him, corruption cannot be so easily eradicated unless people and those who are in power. If there is no probity in the public life of individuals, then our lives are not worth living. To quote Gandhi in this context:

---

[9] Gandhi, *Harijan,* May 1939.

[10] Gandhi, *The Hindu,* 27 January 1948.

> It is the duty of all leading men, whatever their persuasion or party, to safeguard the dignity of India. That dignity can't be saved if misgovernment and corruption flourish. Misgovernment and corruption always go together. I have it from very trustworthy sources that corruption is increasing in our country. Is everyone then going to think only of himself, and not to all of India?[11]

Lack of commitment, honesty and feeling of brotherhood destroys social harmony and progress. If the people at the helm of affairs are either corrupt, or non-vigilant, or indulgent, or too liberal to deal with corruption, then corruption becomes unstoppable. Certainly the dreams of Gandhi to realize a moral and ethical society would be fast vanishing.

Summary

Like Aristotle and Sri Aurobindo, Gandhi felt that man, society and human values are inseparable from each other. One cannot think of man without society and society without man. Similarly, there is no society without human values. They regulate our moral conduct in the society. Lack of moral values breeds corruption and it is a progenitor of poverty, terror and other threats affecting social harmony and progress. Greed in any form is highly condemnable. Corruption debases human values and encourages the traits of a demon such as greed, conceit, deceit, self-centredness, hatred, malice, dishonesty, lack of responsibility and concern for others' needs and so on. The drastic increase in the corrupt practices and the collapse of norms for running the affairs of nation are of immediate concern to any sensible individual. We need to detoxify our public life and every individual has his or her responsibility to tackle this problem. What Gandhi said nearly six decades ago sounds more apt for the contemporary society. People from all walks of life must realize that corruption slowly

---

[11] Gandhi, *The Hindu*, 16 December 1947.

eats away our moral values and reduces us to the level of barbarians. Our commitment to minimize corruption, as it is impossible to root it out completely, must come from within. As Amartya Sen rightly observed, the empowerment of women, education and health care are the three important features of any welfare society. If we are unable to extend these minimum things to the citizens of our nation in spite of the fact that we achieved independence way back in 1947, it only shows that there is something wrong with our social policies. It is not too late for us to come back to our normal senses to realize the negative impact of corruption in fulfilling our dreams for an egalitarian society.

5

Economic Philosophy

NOT ONLY our country, but the entire globe is witnessing an unprecedented economic slowdown. According to economists and market experts, the situation is going to be much worse in coming months and years. Unless we take firm steps to curb inflation, the life of common man would be miserable and pathetic. The popular belief is that there is tremendous progress in almost all fronts of human life. This may be true for a small section of people, but not to all. Deaths due to hunger, lack of proper nourishment, and lack of health care are increasing day by day. A welfare society is one in which there is promotion and protection of economic and social well-being of all its citizens. Equal opportunities and equal distribution of nation's wealth to all its citizens would be the preamble of any ideal welfare society. Modern economic models to a great extent failed to protect the right to livelihood of millions of individuals all over the globe. Exploitation of individuals and natural resources has become the order of the day for modern industrialized economy. The modern industrialized economy contributed to the lopsided development of so-called advanced societies wherein the division between the rich and poor is widening. In the name of urbanization, the village or rural economy is completely ignored. Under these circumstances, we have to go back to Gandhian economic model which promotes the socio-economic growth of every individual as a citizen of a welfare society.

An attempt is made in this chapter to assess whether Gandhian economic model would be a viable alternative to modern economic theories for overall development of nation's economy and well-being of its citizens.

Gandhian Model

Of course, people are sceptical about the relevance of Gandhian economic model in the twenty-first century, for it is outdated and obsolete. Is it really so? The basic human needs for a dignified existence of any human being are food, clothing and shelter. However advanced the human societies are in terms of civilization, if the basic needs of human beings are not take care of, then all our claims to advancement in any sphere are mere empty claims. For Gandhi, the first priority is to alleviate exploitation of both human and natural resources and poverty. Such a goal calls for reorganization of socio-economic structure. He identified the decadence in moral values as the root cause of the downfall of any socio-economic order. Thus economics and morality go hand in hand for Gandhi. His economic philosophy is the outcome of the modern challenges faced by people due to strains of capitalism and communalism.[1] Gandhi felt that production must be determined by the social necessity rather than the greed of a section of people. If genuine social needs of people are neglected, then there is no social progress. The expression "social progress" is a comprehensive term in Gandhian philosophy. It encapsulates everything that is worthy of dignified human existence. Gandhian approach to economic order is essentially revolutionary and constructive. He introduced a novel idea called trusteeship. According to him, the idea of trusteeship would open up harmonious relationship between the employer and employee. The existing economic inequalities are the result of the lack of trust between the employer and the employee. They are the two sides of the

---

[1] Das 1979: 327.

same coin. Both the employer and the employee must be bound by moral values in the sense that they must realize their duties as obligations. Thus moral values are the backbone for any progressive society. To quote Gandhi in this context:

> Economic equality is the master key to non-violent independence. Working for economic equality means abolishing the eternal conflict between capital and labour. It means the levelling down of the few rich in whose hands is concentrated the bulk of the nation's wealth on the one hand, and the levelling up of the semi-starved naked millions on the other . . . a non-violent system of government is clearly an impossibility, so long as the wide gulf between the rich and the hungry millions persists. . . .[2]

The above passage clearly shows that the economic inequality is the root cause of violence. Unless and until it is rooted out, the eternal conflict between the rich and the poor continues to exist. The rich must come forward to share their riches for the benefit of common good. This moral and emotional appeal of Gandhi was ridiculed by his critics. His critics felt that economic order and moral order do not influence each other. They are like parallel lines. But Gandhi is against such a view. He viewed that people can acquire personal property under certain moral conditions. Modern economic models give utmost importance to the capital than to the labour. Gandhi gives importance to labour over capital. In the absence of labour nothing can be moulded into a finer product of human consumption. Gandhi is right in saying so. However, to invoke polar argument here, both capital and labour are interdependent in any developing society. Exploitation of workers' labour by the capitalists and unrealistic demands of workers by paralyzing the production are equally unjustifiable. According to Gandhi, it is through nonviolence total economic

---

[2] Gandhi 1944: 20-21.

reforms can be brought about for the benefit of everyone. For a proper harmony between capital and labour, Gandhi envisaged trusteeship as an ideal arrangement. Gandhi did not really support private ownership of capital which is used by the individuals for their selfish benefits. Instead his trusteeship aimed at transforming the existing capital order into an egalitarian society.[3] Capitalists have to become the trustees for the welfare of the labouring class. The capital is meant for the economic and moral welfare of the labouring class.[4] Gandhi always believed that he can appeal to the capitalists to realize that the capital possessed by them is the fruit of the labouring class. Therefore, held Gandhi:

> I am inviting those people who consider themselves as owners today to act as trustees, i.e., owners, not in their own right, but owners in the right of those whom they have exploited.[5]

This statement of Gandhi makes us realize that Gandhi heavily relied on conscience. It is the real catalyst for him to transform any society into a welfare society. A person who amassed huge wealth either by means of legacy or by trade and business must know that the entire wealth does not belong to him. What is necessary must be utilized by him for a good and honourable living and the rest must be used for the welfare of the community. The privileged classes must outgrow their greed and selfish interests for the betterment of the labouring class. Gandhi was optimistic about his proposal and believed that the trusteeship would definitely work. Even if it fails, it is not that the theory is false or wrong but it is the weakness of the wealthy which makes trusteeship false.[6]

---

[3] Ray 1969: 8.

[4] Gandhi, *Young India*, 20 August 1925.

[5] Ibid., 26 November 1931.

[6] Gandhi, *Harijan*, 16 November 1939.

Trusteeship and Economic Order

Gandhi's idea of trusteeship was made more practical and simple by Kishore Lal Mashruwala and Narahari Parikh. According to them, the objective of trusteeship is to transform the capitalist economic order into an egalitarian society. Such a transformation gradually removes capitalism by giving the capitalists to reform themselves. Second, trusteeship does not encourage any right to private property. Even if property is owned by the individual(s) it is owned for the benefit of community's welfare. Third, it is within the legislative regulation of ownership and use of wealth. Fourth, the property, which is under the control of state-regulated trusteeship, cannot be used by an individual for his selfish benefits. Fifth, there must be a fixed maximum income for any individual in a society. He or she cannot possess more than what is allowed by the state. The difference between the minimum income for decent living and the maximum income allowed for an individual must be within the permissible limits. Sixth, the character of production must be determined by the social necessity but not by individual choice or greed.[7]

Gandhi's entire exercise in this direction is intended to promote equal distribution of wealth through nonviolence. In order to realize this goal every individuals needs to make certain necessary changes in one's personal life. We have to cut down our desires and wants keeping in view the poor economic condition of the nation. Self-control and self-restraint are the basic ingredients of trusteeship. The doctrine of equal distribution works out well, according to Gandhi, only when the affluent realize that part of their wealth needs to be shared with the poor in order to improve their living standards. But, is it possible? Do the capitalists realize their responsibility? Similarly, the poor must realize that the rich cannot accumulate

---

[7] Gandhi, *Harijan*, 25 October 1952.

their disproportionate assets without the cooperation of the poor. As rightly observed by K.S. Murty, Gandhi's "doctrine of trusteeship means the use of all one has, for the good of all".[8]

Economic Equality

Does trusteeship pave the way for economic equality? Of course, Gandhi is aware of the limitations of his doctrine. Economic equality in his view is not the absolute equality. He clarified his views on economic equality in the following manner:

> Economic equality must never be supposed to mean possession of an equal amount of worldly goods by everyone. It does not mean, however, that everyone will have a proper house to live in, sufficient and balanced food to eat, and sufficient *khadi* with which to cover himself. It also means that the cruel inequality that obtains today will be removed by purely non-violent means.[9]

According to Gandhi,

> a good *satyāgrahī* is one who leads simple life with great honesty. He should handle public funds more carefully as he is accountable with utmost care. This is the first step towards a healthy life in society. A *satyāgrahī* must come forward to sacrifice his precious life and possessions for the welfare of the community.[10]

To quote Gandhi in this context:

> I shall bring about economic equality through non-violence, by converting the people to my point of view. . . . I will not wait till I have converted the whole society to my view but will straight away make a beginning with my self. . . . For

---

[8] Murty 1982: 111.

[9] Gandhi, *Harijan,* 18 August 1940.

[10] Gandhi 1951: 73.

> that I have to reduce myself to the level of the poorest of the poor.[11]

This above statement of Gandhi is highly insightful. He did not want to wait for others to follow him rather he wanted to go ahead with his commitment as he felt it right to do so. This is where Gandhi differed from other great social reformers. The only way to root out inequality is to commit oneself to fight inequality in society. The talented lot must utilize their intelligence for better economic possessions. Similarly, they should also use their talents for the better economic welfare of all people. Gandhi held that:

> I would allow a man of intelligent to earn more, I would not cramp his talent, But the bulk of his greater earnings must be used for the good of state, Just as the income of the all earnings of sons of the father go to the common family fund. They would have their earnings only as trustees.[12]

To share one's riches with the others requires a sense of courage to sacrifice. It is possible only when we have empathy with the poor. We must imagine ourselves in the situation of poor. Only then we can know what the poverty means. It is not mere sympathy that leads to sacrifice, but it is empathy which transforms an individual into an ideal man. Spirit of renunciation and raising above one's own self are the necessary prerequisites on the part of every individual to strive to contribute to the economic equality. What is required for frugal and dignified living must be kept and the rest must be utilized for the community's welfare. Gandhi advised that people must adjust themselves to balanced diet and can possess a liveable accommodation. They can also possess wealth for the purpose of children's education and health care.[13]

---

[11] Gandhi, *Harijan*, 25 March 1946.

[12] Gandhi, *Young India*, 26 November 1931.

[13] Gandhi, *Harijan*, 31 March 1946.

Beyond that an individual is not supposed to possess anything. It is not by means of force or violence, but through rational appeal and love there can be transformation in the society. In fact, Gandhi realized that it is not possible to promote equal distribution. Therefore, it recommended equitable distribution. In other words, "to each according to his need" is the fundamental objective of equitable distribution. Gandhi defined economic equality in the following manner:

> The real implications of equal distribution is that each man shall have the wherewithal to supply all his natural needs and no more. For example, if one man has a weak digestion and requires only a quarter of a pound of flour for his bread and another needs a pound, both should be in a position to satisfy their wants. To bring this ideal into being, the entire social order has got to be reconstructed. A society based on nonviolence cannot nurture any other ideal. We cannot perhaps be able to realize the goal, but we must bear it in mind and work unceasingly to near it. To the same extent as we progress towards our goal, we shall find contentment and happiness.[14]

Of course, Gandhi is very clear about his definition of economic equality. He knew that it is not all that easy to achieve it. It requires absolute commitment on the part of every individual to near this goal. In other words, every individual has to change one's own lifestyle to suit the desirable social reconstruction. Therefore, it becomes a collective activity. The success of any collective activity is dependent upon the commitment of the individuals who are responsible for making collective activity a successful one.

Limits of Industrialization

Gandhi formed a definite view of industrialization of his time from the writings of Ruskin and Tolstoy, who wrote on the

---

[14] Gandhi, *Harijan*, 25 August 1940.

economic history of India under the British rule. The hallmark of industrialization is that machine enslaves man. Slavery, poverty, exploitation and decadent value system are the chief traits of industrialization. It completely ignores the role of village economy. The rapid urbanization prompted labour to migrate from villages to big towns and cities for better wages. Thus it led to the impoverishment of Indian villages.[15] Industrialization promotes large quantities of production. Consequently it requires vast quantities of raw materials and huge sums of capital. In order to sell their finished goods for making profits, the advanced or the developed countries exploit the developing and underdeveloped countries. The result would be:

> Colonial expansion, imperialism, commercial monopoly, repeated war with the rival industrialized countries, diplomatic mechanism for keeping down the economic and political growth of the rivals as well as of the myths of cultural, racial, and religious superiorities of the exploiters — all follow in a ceaseless train, demoralizing to the whole world.[16]

The employment of good number of labourers, and huge capital investment have their own problems. There would be strained relations between the capital and the labour. The mindless use of machinery would certainly affect the moral fabric of any society. Once the values are taken a back seat then there is no respect for human life in such a society. Thus the dehumanizing effects of industrialization sow the seeds of exploitation. Exploitation leads to poverty, accumulation of wealth by a section of people, unemployment and misery. Such a situation slowly breeds violence for there is uneven distribution of wealth. Also, the rapid industrialization

---

[15] Singh, 1988: 153.

[16] Dutta 1953: 112.

contributed to the breakdown in the family relationships. The healthy social and neighbourly relations have lost their significance. Humans are treated as means to serve the ends of a section of humans. Life is reduced to a mechanical drudgery. Thus the whole process of industrialization, according to Gandhi, is a monstrous process of mechanization, dehumanization and demoralization.[17]

Gandhi's views on industrialization almost echo the views of critical theorists. Although we appreciate the progress of scientific rationality (scientific realism) in terms of better science and technology, we regret its progress if it does not accommodate moral rationality (philosophical idealism) which stands for human values. Unless both these dimensions are given equal importance there won't be a proper welfare society. Unfortunately, as noticed by Gandhi, the modern civilization almost ignored the moral rationality. Consequently, it is the quantity that dominates quality of life and mechanism completely ignoring human values. If human being is reduced to the level of a machine then there is no point in talking about humanism. Mass production prompts alienation of individuals not only from the products produced by them but also from their own species. Therefore, the craze for machinery undermines the natural talents and creativity of individuals. Thus human resource takes a back seat in the industrial civilization. The real progress of mankind does not lie in the mere material progress. The most unfortunate thing is that modern industrial civilization does not attach any importance to moral and religious values. Even if it promotes religion, it is only in the interest of the trade. Thus religion practised in the industrialized societies is not a genuine one but only a commercialized form of religion.

Gandhi's objection to the employment of large-scale machinery is not baseless. He openly declared that the large-

---

[17] Dutta 1953: 113.

scale machinery would enrich only a section of people (capitalists) at the cost of the lives of the others. It will also promote unemployment. Gandhi recommended mechanization only when there is a dearth of labourers. But in a country like India there is no dearth for human resource. To quote Gandhi in this context:

> Mechanization is good when hands are too few for the work intended to be accomplished. It is an evil where there are more hands than required for the work, as is the case of India. The problem with us is not how to find leisure for the teeming millions inhabiting our villages. The problem is how to utilize their idle hours, which are equal to the working days of six months in the year.[18]

Gandhi was realistic in his approach to industrialization. His vehement attack on industrialization is not merely an outburst against the modern Western civilization. However, he admitted that if industrialization is on the right track and direction then it would be treated as the fountainhead of prosperity of all. Mass production brings down the prices of commodities. But it will promote massive unemployment. This will also enable the rich to possess wealth for their self-growth. The accumulation of wealth by a group of individuals amounts to unequal distribution of wealth and natural resources. Accumulation of many by a group of individuals is a highly dangerous phenomenon.[19] Concentration of wealth and employment of machinery for the benefit of few is unwelcome for it destroys the livelihood of many. However, machinery which would be beneficial to all is welcome.

It is a mistake to conclude that Gandhi opposed science and technology. He opposed all forms of scientific and technological innovations that benefit industrialists alone.

---

[18] Gandhi, *Harijan*, 16 November 1934.

[19] Gandhi, *Kurukshetra*, October 1994, Annual Number.

Gandhi held that: "machinery has a place; it has come to stay. But it must not be allowed to displace necessary human labour."[20] In a country like India we need only such type of machinery which would be of use to all but not to a few. Technology must be non-exploitative and its purpose is to bring about a radical social change for the benefit of all. We must not substitute technology for human labour. It must be used only to produce such goods or instruments that help the workers. Technology with a human face is welcome so that people love working.[21] Of course, Gandhi admitted that some vital industries are necessary for the economic growth of the nation. But they must be under the control of the state but not with individuals.

Gandhi time and again emphasized that rural industries must be encouraged for they are non-exploitative. The production must be the production of masses. Mass production by the large-scale industrial units mainly target the wants of people but not their genuine needs. Needs of people have to be prioritized by a welfare society. Wants should not overwhelm the needs. People who give preference to their wants over the needs of people are incapable of realizing higher values. Therefore, "high thinking is inconsistent with material life".[22] Negligence of rural economy and village structure would destroy the normal life of individuals. For our day-to-day survival we need food grains, pulses, vegetables, fruits and dairy products. They are necessary for human survival. There is no point in producing huge quantities of cloth, steel or any other non-consumable thing when people are struggling to get a square meal a day. Survival of man is the priority. Therefore, what is needed for the dignified living of human beings must be prioritized. In fact, the concept of rural

---

[20] Gandhi, *Young India*, 5 January 1925.

[21] Schumacher 1973: 18.

[22] Gandhi, *Harijan*, 1 September 1946.

development envisaged by Gandhi is a comprehensive one. It encapsulates the principles of life-sustenance, self-respect and freedom. Food, clothing, shelter, health care and social security are covered by life-sustenance. To live the dignified life comes under self-respect. It is not a mere political ideological freedom, but freedom from social servitude that makes human beings free. All these three are covered under the Gandhian concept of rural development. The ideal of Gandhian economic philosophy is to eliminate poverty, unemployment and dignified life. In that sense economic development is a multi-dimensional affair.

Summary

No one would ever forget the selfless service rendered by Gandhi to the masses of Indian subcontinent. His crusade against poverty, unethical practices, inequality in the social, economic and religious spheres is genuine and committed. Gandhi aimed at abolishing poverty through nonviolent and non-alienated technology which would help labourers maximizing their human dignity. It is only through decentralized pattern can there be any economic regeneration. Equal participation, equal distribution of wealth and natural resources would only establish an egalitarian society. Due importance must be given to rural economy and village structure. Mere industrialization at the cost of rural or village economy would be detrimental to human welfare. The very survival of human race would be under constant threat if industrialization is allowed in its present form where there is no role for human values. The dehumanizing effects of modern civilization reduce a human being to the level of a consumer. In such societies there cannot be justice, freedom and happiness.

Gandhi did not distinguish economy from morality. His emphasis on human values is worth examination. Gandhi felt that a good economic philosophy is based on ethical foundations. Nonviolence, compassion and love must be the constitutive aspects of such ethics. These virtues find their expression not only in the personal lives of individuals but must be extended to political, economic and social life of individuals. An individual is not isolated from community, society, nation and humanity. Individual and society are the two sides of the same coin. Gandhi time and again held that it is the inner voice of individual(s) that guides to a perfect human action. Gandhi is fully convinced that man by nature is good and it is the truth in man. One has to conquer one's passions and emotions in order to cultivate self-discipline. In that sense Gandhi was a perfect idealist.

However, Gandhian economic philosophy has its limitations. He realized towards the end of the British rule that his philosophy can be practised only at the individual level. Unfortunately, the realistic world is not what Gandhi wanted it to be. In contemporary politics we witness the power of money and muscle over the power of goodwill. Human values are least respected and almost thrown overboard. Violence has obliterated nonviolence. The former is real and the latter is only an ideal or an utopian notion. Greed, covetousness, conceit, deceit, nepotism, corruption, self-aggrandisement, exploitation have become the order of the day. On the contrary, sincerity, loyalty, commitment, dedication and honesty have become rare commodities. Therefore, Gandhian economic philosophy which is rooted in the basic human values does not work in the contemporary world. When current social practices go against the established moral norms then there is a need to reframe the latter in the light of the former. Our new social structure, perhaps, does not allow the old and traditional ways of thinking as the real guiding spirit. At the most the Gandhian ideals can be practised at the individual level but not at social level. Let us not deceive ourselves by claiming to be Gandhians. Why is India not able to surge ahead, socially or economically, in spite of the fact that we claim to follow the ideals of Gandhi? The gap between the rich and poor, urban and rural is widening day by day. Gandhi's philosophy served the purpose some seven decades ago. In the twentieth century Gandhi's miracle does not work. Gandhi would have realized the limitations of his own philosophy, if he were to live today.

6

Socialist Outlook
Gandhi and Marx

Are Gandhi (1869–1948) and Marx (1818-83) forgotten heroes? Have their doctrines any relevance in the contemporary society? Where do their doctrines stand in the contemporary socio-political scenario? The socio-political ideals advanced by both Gandhi and Marx cannot be simply dubbed as utopian ideals, for they are not dreamers. The social philosophies of Gandhi and Marx suggest that they are not mere visionaries of their times, but great social reformers. The former directly participated in the social movements in India and the latter's teachings served as a catalyst for many a social reform across the globe. In fact, there are some unexplored similarities between these two great visionaries. In their social philosophies both Gandhi and Marx recognized "social conflict" as a fact. The conflict between the capitalist and labourer, landlord and cultivator is accepted by them. Apart from this conflict, Gandhi also noticed another conflict between city (urban) and village where the terms of trade offered for food and raw materials by the former were exploitative. Like Marx, Gandhi too felt that there must a stronger mechanism to put down exploitation. Therefore, there is a need to invoke stronger forces in human nature to meet this end. Both are opposed to exploitation of every kind. But they adopted different methods to curb exploitation. Gandhi envisaged that non-cooperation and passive resistance by the exploited against the exploiters would bring down this social evil and cultivate the idea of "trusteeship" among the owners of land and capital. On the contrary, Marx envisaged that it is the violent proletariat revolt against the exploiters would bring down this social menace. Unlike Marx, Gandhi allowed individual ownership in so far as the owner himself directly used the property or worked on it. In this chapter an attempt is made to compare and contrast the two distinguished socialists belonging to two different social situations. Gandhi's socialism is mainly aimed at establishing the social justice in an agrarian society while that of Marx is aimed at an industrialized society.

The Socialist Ideology of Gandhi

As a matter of fact, moral and spiritual principles have direct bearing on Gandhi's social, political and economic ideals. He sharply reacted to the exploitation of human individuals under capitalism. His concern for downtrodden and economically poorer sections of society made him condemn the exploitative nature of capitalist regime. He always wished that decent life and satisfactory standards of living must be extended to all human beings alike. Human welfare or common good is the sole criterion for Gandhi to judge any economic system or institution. Gandhi viewed all our property relations from an ethical point of view. In this context he wrote:

> I suggest that we are thieves in a way. If I take anything that I do not need for my own immediate use, and keep it, I thieve it from somebody else. . . .[1]

Thus Gandhi's rejection of capitalism solely rests on ethical grounds. The living conditions of the poor can be improved by changing the existing socio-economic structure. The only way to safeguard the interests of poor and needy is to throw capitalism out. Gandhi opposed the British imperialists of

---

1 Bose 1972: 60.

his time for imposing poverty on the Indian masses. He equally criticized the Indian capitalists for exploiting their fellow compatriots. In fact, Gandhi's purity of means prevented him from taking any drastic step to curb capitalism. In this context Gandhi wrote:

> Socialism is as pure as crystal. It, therefore, requires crystal-like means to achieve it. Impure means results in an impure end. Hence the prince and the peasant will not be equalized by cutting prince's head. . . . Only truthful, nonviolent and pure-hearted socialists will be able to establish a socialist society in India and the world.[2]

The influence of Christianity on Gandhi is so conspicuous when he quotes the saying of the Christ:

> Man cannot live on bread alone. But it is also a fact that he cannot live without it either. However superior the spirit may be than matter, the spirit manifests itself in man through his flesh.[3]

Although Gandhi advised people to reduce their wants, yet there is a need for some amount of material goods for a decent life. Certain amount of material comforts are required for man, for otherwise what is the difference between man and lower creatures. Gandhi held that

> No one has ever suggested that grinding pauperism can lead to anything else than moral degradation.[4]

But Gandhi also warned people not to nurture unwanted desires and wants. What is required to keep oneself happy at the minimal level is welcomed by him.

Economic wealth is something that is socially produced. It cannot be produced by any individual in isolation from

---

[2] Gandhi, *Harijan*, 13 July 1947.

[3] Kripalani 1970: 367.

[4] Bose 1972: 76.

society. Therefore, it must be equally divided among all men. The basic necessities of life have to be made freely available to all. Just as water and air are God's commodities which are accessible to every one of us, so also all the basic necessities must be provided to all. The monopolization of the basic necessities by a nation or a group individuals is treated unjust by Gandhi. The neglect of this simple principle is the cause of destitution which is witnessed today. Gandhi opined:

> Nature produces enough for our wants from day-to-day, and if everybody took enough for himself and nothing more, there would be no pauperism in this world, there would be no man dying of starvation in this world.[5]

Gandhi makes no distinction between economics and ethics. Genuine economics, for Gandhi, stands for "social justice" and moral values. The economics that disregards moral values only breeds injustice and social ill-will. True economics is indispensable for good society and for a decent life of the individuals. Gandhi held that:

> I must confess that I do not draw as sharp or any distinction between economics and ethics. Economics that hurt the moral well-being of an individual or a nation is immoral and therefore sinful.[6]

Gandhi makes it clear that socialism was not born to discover the misuse of capital by the capitalists. Both socialism and communism were explicit in the first verse of *Īśopaniṣad.* Scientific socialism was born when some reforms lost faith in the method of conversion. In his discussion with Luis Fischer, Gandhi explained the differences between him and others as regards the notion of socialism. He maintained that:

---

[5] Bose 1972: 75.

[6] Gandhi, *Young India,* 20 November 1921.

> My socialism means "even unto the last". I do not want to rise on the ashes of the blind, the deaf and the dumb. In their socialism, probably these have no place. Their one aim is material progress . . . I do not . . . I want freedom for full expression of my personality. . . . Under the other socialism, there is no individual freedom.[7]

Gandhi argued that everyone must be provided with sufficient work to enable oneself to make his both ends meet. This ideal must be universally recognized. The means of production must necessarily be in the hands of masses but not with capitalists. He believed that mass-production of commodities by using machinery is responsible for the present world crisis. Mass-production of commodities by machines is concentrated only in particular areas. And the regulation of distribution is done roundabout way. On the other hand, Gandhi suggested that production must be localized where things are required, then distribution is automatically regulated. Consequently, there is less scope for fraud, speculation and hoarding. Therefore, instead of mass-production on machinery, Gandhi recommended for the production by the masses "in peoples own homes". This will avoid the concentration of production in the hands of the few.

Coming to Gandhi's views on use of machinery and industrialism, initially he opposed all forms of machinery. But he realized that "machinery has its place; it has come to stay. But it must not be allowed to displace necessary human labour."[8] There is a reason why Gandhi opposed machinery in the beginning. During the pre-Independence times most of the people were without work. Then Gandhi felt that when there is plenty of human resource available why cannot we use it in the place of machinery. However, he also hinted at

---

[7] Gandhi, *Harijan,* 4 August 1946.

[8] Gandhi, *Young India,* 20 November 1924.

that there must be improvement in our domestic machinery which would hasten the work of the individual by lessening his labour. Gandhi held that:

> I am uncompromisingly against all destructive machinery. But simple tools and instruments and such machinery as saves individual labour and lightens the burden of the millions of cottages, I should welcome.[9]

Therefore, there is an apparent change in his attitude towards machinery. He moved from "no machine" to "small machine". Gandhi was not opposed to machinery, but one must not be crazy of machines which rob people of their daily wages and life. Machinery in the hands of capitalists promotes concentration of wealth in few hands. This is not good for any welfare society.

Gandhi's *sarvodaya* is an important preamble to socialism. It seeks the welfare of all. Since all men are born equal no one must be treated as a stranger to another or superior to another. Therefore, the welfare of all human beings must be the motto of true socialism. Gandhi's socialism is an extension of economic aspect of *sarvodaya*. In his socialism everyone is equal in the sense equal opportunities are provided to all. There is no difference between a prince and a peasant, wealthy and poor, employer and employee. *Sarvodya* is a superior concept than "utilitarianism". And he claimed that it is even superior to the Marxist socialism which is restricted to the welfare of proletariat only. But Gandhi missed a point here. In a Marxist socialist state there is no capitalist. Ultimately everyone is reduced to a proletariat. Therefore, Marx envisaged the socialism of proletariat.

What are the means to socialism? Gandhi held that "means and ends are convertible terms". They are inseparable and interdependent. Therefore both means and ends must have

---

[9] Ibid., 17 June 1926.

same purity. The purity of a tree lies in the purity of the seed from which it gets actualized. Potentially the seed is good so the tree which is actualized from the seed is also pure. Since the end grows out of means we can only control the means but not the end. As it is held in *Gītā,* the good deeds result in good ends, for Gandhi good means end in good consequences (ends). To quote Gandhi in this context:

> Means to be means must always be within our reach and *ahiṁsā* is our supreme duty. If we take care of the means, we bound to reach the end sooner or later.[10]

Gandhi's aversion to violence, coercion and force made him an anti-communist. Although he admired the spirit of sacrifice of his communist friends, he could not agree with their method and said:

> They frankly believed in violence and all that is in bosom.[11]

On the contrary, he held that:

> My socialism was natural to me and adopted from the books. It came out of my unshakable belief in non-violence. . . . Unfortunately Western socialists have, so far as I know, believed in the necessity of violence for enforcing socialist doctrines.[12]

Gandhi admitted that he was not well acquainted with the scientific form of socialism. According to him, it is not a suitable form of socialism to Indian people. He always insisted on right means to arrive at right ends. His right means always presuppose nonviolence as a virtue. If any means to achieve any end bypasses this principle of nonviolence, then it is treated as impure means. For Gandhi, nonviolence is righteousness.

---

10 Bose 1972: 14.

11 Gandhi, *Harijan,* 4 August 1946.

12 Ibid., 20 April 1940.

The Socialist Ideology of Marx

Karl Marx is another crusader of human freedom in his own right. His doctrine of political economy transformed the mindset and lifestyle of millions of people all over the world. Several nations adopted his socialist ideology to bring about social revolutions. But Marx's approach to socialism is diametrically opposed to Gandhian approach. Like Gandhi, Marx too held that under the capitalist regime common man is completely neglected and his welfare has taken a back seat. Through his historical materialism Marx identified the socio-historical factors that lead to private ownership, means of production, surplus value, domination of the rich over the poor. He visualized that in the long run, capitalism is going to collapse due to inherent internal contradictions within itself. What Marx viewed is that scientific socialism is not an accidental doctrine rather it is inbuilt in the very social nature. The contradictions between the owners and working class, the appropriator and the producer, the exploiter and the exploited clearly establish the view that there is no smooth sail for capitalism.

Unlike Gandhi, Marx did not base his socialism on moral or spiritual grounds. Socialism's success is dependent only on a scientific explanation. The materialistic interpretation of history and the secrets of capitalist mode of production paved the way for scientific socialism. However, Marx admitted that capitalism is a necessary stage for socialism. The capitalist mode of production gives rise to alienation of three kinds.

1. The producer is alienated from what is produced by him. What is produced by him is appropriated by the capitalist.
2. The producer expends his labour to produce something. In return he does not get back full worth of his labour in terms of economy. Since labour is the

essential element of every human being, he is alienated from his own labour, the essential element.

3. In the process of production each one is engaged in his task of producing something. Thus every individual is isolated from the other individuals.

This amounts to the alienation of the producer from his own species. Marx recognized these three forms of alienation. Regarding the capitalist mode of production Marx held that:

> It creates those material conditions which alone can form the real basis of a higher form of society, a society in which the full and free development of every individual forms the ruling principle.[13]

Of course, a capitalist economy provides us with all the necessary infrastructure for the development of new socialist society by its intensive development and centralization of industry, rationalization of techniques of production, concentration of capital and socialization of production, etc.

Marx's conception of social development is dialectical. Each stage of social development is rooted in its earlier forms and evolves out of the process of opposition and disharmony. Therefore every stage in the social development is treated as qualitatively new. These inherent laws that underlie, while the process of social development can be empirically analysed, according to Marx. In the capitalist mode of production, the capitalist is the gainer and he becomes more and more rich. While the working class which toils for the benefit of the capitalist remains in the same condition. According to Marx:

> Centralization of the means of production and socialization of labour at last reach a point where they become incompatible with their capitalist integument. Thus integument is burst asunder.[14]

---

13 Marx 1867: 555.

14 Ibid.: 715.

Marx observed that the material conditions that transformed capitalism into socialism were present in capitalism itself. Thus socialism is an inevitable product of capitalism. In support of Marx's view Lenin wrote:

> There is no trace of utopianism in Marx, in the sense that he made up or invented a "new society". No, he studied the birth of a new society out of the old, and the forms of transition from the latter to the former, as a natural historical process.[15]

Marx envisaged the dictatorship of the proletariat in the socialist state. In the struggle between the old ruling class and the emerging new class (proletariat class) the latter gets strengthened in its struggle. Consequently, capitalism gets defeated and new socialist order would be established. The dictatorship of the proletariat is a necessary step for establishing a classless society, according to Marx. The dictatorship of the proletariat does not mean that there is an authority of a single person resulting in demolishing all norms of democracy. But it is based on the democratic principles of the majority rule. It is qualitatively a new type of state and a better form of democracy than that of capitalism. Marx opposed any attempt to perfecting the bourgeois state mechanism. Instead he recommended its destruction as it is based on class structure. Marx realized that in all the past revolutions in France, the revolutionaries tried to perfect the state machinery. This is the mistake committed by them. They must have smashed it completely. The working class must create its own state machine in the form of dictatorship of the proletariat so that it can carry out its socialist reforms.

The First Phase of Communism

The first phase of communism is an outcome of the socialism.

---

15 Lenin: 1917: 425.

In its nascent form it would be incomplete in many respects as it is a natural outcome of capitalism. To quote Marx in this context:

> . . . it emerges from the capitalist society: which is thus in every respect; economically, morally and intellectually, still stamped with the birth marks of the old society from whose womb it emerges.[16]

Under socialist state the affairs of the society have to be followed on the principle of "each according to his ability, to each according to his work". It lays down the foundation stone for a new set of human relations. Of course, at this stage one cannot expect economic equality, and human needs are reduced to basic minimum existence. Therefore, Marx himself called such a state of communism "crude communism". In this state every man becomes a working man and productive labour ceases to be a class attribute.

Abolition of Private Property

In a capitalist society private ownership is allowed and it becomes the prerogative of the capitalist class. But in a socialist state private property becomes a collective product of all individuals. It is the private property, according to Marx, which creates a sense of ego in the individual. And this ego is the source of discrimination and exploitation. In socialist state the ownership of means of production is abolished and it becomes the property of all the citizens of the state. Marx and Engels made it clear that

> communism deprives no man of the power to appropriate the products of society; all that it does is to deprive him of the power to subjugate the labour of others by means of such appropriation.[17]

---

[16] Marx, 1970: 17.

[17] Marx and Engels, 1969: 66.

Communism does not abolish the appropriation of one's fruits of labour. Such an appropriation is necessary to maintain the day-to-day life of the individuals. But it does not allow any surplus that would command the labour of the others.

Under capitalist regime there is bound to be economic inequality. But in a communist state there is economic equality. Those who contribute to the values of the world are recognized and rewarded in a communist state. There is no poverty and one does not have any dearth of basic needs that are required for a dignified human existence. Equality, according to Marx, is to abolish special privileges to certain individuals. Elimination of class distinctions is the first step towards economic equality. Marxian socialism abolishes the opposition between mental and manual labour. It will destroy the ruling class's hegemony and monopoly of state's economic share. There is no distinction between city and village. Everyone is guaranteed equal opportunity. No one is deprived of any right in so far as it is the right of the human being.

Summary

To conclude, both Gandhi and Marx opposed exploitation of masses by any economically powerful individual or a group. Gandhi preferred nonviolent path to achieve his goal whereas Marx preferred revolution through violence to transform the capitalist society into a socialist order. Both Gandhi and Marx predicted that free competition in unequal world shall create ever larger monopolies and consequently, capitalists and imperialists in various conations after garnering capital at home, will intensify colonization of the Third World countries. Such a trend leads to intense colonial-imperialist wars. Unfortunately the society evolved today keeps a distance from the ideals of Gandhi and Marx. Although some of the predictions of Gandhi and Marx came true, capitalist resistance to other forms of social structure is so conspicuous. It is not that easy to wipe out capitalism. It is manifesting in the form of imperialism and soft-totalitarianism. The pervasive phenomenon called globalization re-established the supremacy of capitalist world order. The developed countries have tricked the working class by co-opting them into the capitalist structure. The Gandhi–Marx hypothesis that the middle classes would be pushed to pauperization and will join the hands of working class to revolt against capitalism is proved false. Most of the strong socialist states crumbled. The contemporary social scenario in our own nation and elsewhere indicates that moral values have taken a back seat. Self-aggrandisement is the order of the day. Neither the followers of Gandhi nor the followers of Marx could challenge capitalism which is manifesting in the form of soft-totalitarianism. The youth today are more attracted to consumerism and leisure. They lack revolutionary spirit to bring about any radical change in the society. The need is to educate the young to distinguish between genuine and false needs. Our attraction to the latter makes consumerism dominate our lifestyle.

7

Reappraising Gandhi

THE PRESENT chapter is a review of an interesting book *Reading and Reappraising Gandhi* by Ram Chandra Pradhan. When I reviewed this book I found it fascinating for it takes into account the art of interpretation as its central issue. As a student of philosophy I always felt that interpretation always throws ample light on the issues which are hidden or neglected. Thus the art of interpretation paves the way for meaningful debates in philosophy. The author of the book feels that Gandhiana is no more a virgin field, rather it is over-cultivated. Therefore, the onus lies on the author to state something new in the present work in order to make it worthy of reading. The present work is classified into five well-developed parts apart from appendices.

I

The present work is basically concerned with the various theories of interpretation which include both textual and contextual approaches to interpretation. Also, there is a special focus on the interpretations of Quentin Skinner and Terence Ball. Of course, the art of interpretation differs from writer to writer. The author was apparently fascinated and influenced by the remarks of Quentin Skinner and Terence Ball regarding interpretation. According to the former:

> To understand what a writer may have been doing in using some particular concept or argument, we need first of all to

> grasp the nature and range of things that could recognizably have been done by using that particular concept, in the treatment of that particular theme, at that particular time. We need, in short, to be ready to take as our province . . . the complete range of the inherited symbols and representations that constitute the subjectivity of an age.[1]

Similarly, Terence Ball held that:

> Interpretation is not an option but a necessity for the meaning-seeking creatures that we are. . . . Our prehistoric ancestors interpreted the meaning of animal entrails, omens and other signs that might make their future. They, like modern meteorologists, attempted to forecast the weather by looking at clouds and observing the behaviour of birds and other creatures.[2]

Interpretation is the strength of any text. In the Indian context, *bhāṣyakāras* performed the role of interpreters.

Interpretation is not something unique. There are types of interpretation such as Marxian, feminist, deconstructionist and hermeneutical. Further, there are textual and contextual approaches to interpretation. According to the author, the textual approach is basically a closed and sensitive reading of the text in question. However, the author identifies the limitations of the textual interpretation. As observed by Leo Strauss, the interpretation of any classical text requires a good background in philosophy. Since classical texts possess both temporal (historical) and timeless (eternal) truths, it is not all that easy for an interpreter to hold the entire text as absolute and timeless. There is another significant approach called contextual approach. This approach tries to interpret the given text in the light of existing socio–cultural–historical context.

---

1 Pradhan 2011: 1.

2 Ibid.

Since this approach is context specific it does not hold good for all contexts. If every concept is interpreted in terms of a given context then the seminal ideas like "justice", "liberty", "right", "consent" and "obligation" lose their intrinsic worth.

According to the author, Skinner is a well-known political theorist. His important essay on "Meaning and Understanding of History" clearly reflects his views on art of interpretation and throws new light on textual interpretation. In this context Skinner talks about several types of mythologies which go against the rational historical interpretation of any text. The three most important mythologies are:

1. **mythology of doctrines**, according to which while interpreting a text several doctrines are credited to the author and the text even when those doctrines do not exist in reality,
2. **mythology of coherence**, according to which while interpreting a text an attempt is made by the interpreter to find coherence or consistency in the ideas advocated by the author as well as the text where such a coherence is non-existent, and
3. **mythology of prolepsis**, according to which a speaker anticipates and answers the objections and questions raised by one who follows him. This mythology gets its prominence, according to Skinner, when there is a difference between actual historical meaning attached to an episode and its alleged significance perceived by a subsequent interpreter.

Skinner also highlights the dangers of parochialism in the textual approach. The misdescription of a text occurs when one tries to interpret an alien culture and unfamiliar conceptual schema. There is also another possibility of committing to parochialism when one tries to misuse his vantage point in describing the sense of a given work. In fact, Skinner's own methodology of interpretation suggests that the contextual interpretation alone frees us from all these mythologies. In the process, Skinner takes recourse to linguistic context, ontological hermeneutics advanced by Martin Heidegger, Jürgen Habermas and Hans-Georg Gadamer. In addition, he feels that the speech–act theory advocated by John Langshaw Austin and others would also be helpful in bringing out the connection between speech and action. However, Skinner's approach has its own inherent weaknesses. According to Kenneth Minogue, it cannot be applied to all social sciences, especially to political thought. Terence Ball also criticizes Skinner for giving undue importance to the intention of the author.

The author devotes sufficient space for discussing Ball's views on interpretation as he is another well-known political theorist. Ball takes up the issue why one needs to study a classic. According to him, one group believes that studying a classic is an intellectual luxury and extravagance. The other group does not accept this view. One of the proponents of the textualist school is Leo Strauss. The followers of this school believe that classics deserve a careful study for they contain timeless and dateless wisdom. Ball does not support either of these groups for they take extreme positions. Both textualism and contextualism have their own role to play in interpreting a text. But they need to be used scrupulously. While accepting the significance of interpretation, Ball holds the view that in spite of the problems faced by the interpreters at various levels one cannot escape from interpretation. In the absence of interpretation one would not understand any text. Ball also takes into account the interests of the interpreter. Somehow the interests of the interpreter are conspicuous when a text is interpreted. Every interpretation has its advantages and disadvantages, yet each one of them is value laden. Ball observes that there are types of interpretations such as Marxist, Neo-Marxist, Post-structuralist, Deconstructionist, Straussian and New Cambridge history group. Although Ball does not reject the intention of the author, he claims that interpretation has to go beyond it in order to get the response of the reader. Ball's five point strategy of interpretation is as follows:

1. Every interpreter has to make an appropriate choice as regards the method of interpretation.
2. The sources of interpretative problems might include contemporary, historical, literary, logical and philosophical. The interpretative problem serves as a vantage point. Accordingly, the method of interpretation can be adopted.
3. A text to be interpreted must be looked at from the context of composition and the context of reception.
4. An interpreter must foresee how an interpretation could throw light on the contemporary issues.
5. The concern of an interpreter is to achieve a pluralist and problem-centric approach to interpretation.

II

This part deals with the ideas of *Hind Swaraj.* The author presents a summary and centennial view of *Hind Swaraj* for it is most central to the writings of Gandhi. It is a classic by itself for it contains a critique of modernity. The various religious, cultural and intellectual sources shaped Gandhi's psyche and personality. *Rāmāyaṇa, Bhagavad-Gītā* and Buddhism had lasting influence on Gandhi. *Hind Swaraj* is a book written in a dialogical form containing twenty chapters. The aim of the book is to provide a substantial critique of modern civilization. Gandhi targeted modern civilization for promoting "bodily happiness" and "bodily welfare". All the modern techniques of science and technology have a dehumanizing effect. The life of workers is worse than that of beasts under modern civilization. In modern civilization machinery rules the roost.

The British rule in India turned it into an irreligious country. The railways helped the British to establish their might over the Indians. The Hindu–Muslim dissensions also helped the British to establish their supremacy. The modern civilization is like a poisonous *upas* tree which destroys everything surrounding it. The English education system introduced in India by the British is a "false education" system. Gandhi felt that mere transfer of power from the British to the Indians does not bring about true *swaraj* (self-rule). The true *swaraj* calls for individual self-rule and *swaraj* as the home rule. The passive resistance based on "love-force" and "soul-force" would establish true *swaraj*. Also, *Hind Swaraj* inculcates the concept of Indian nationalism in the minds of people. Irrespective of their religious differences people retain their national identity. This is the hallmark of nationalism. Non-interference in the religious affairs of others would promote the sense of coexistence and mutual respect to each one's religion. A new society can be established only by mastering one's own mind and minimizing the luxuries and pleasures of one's life. Small-scale technologies and decentralized polity would usher in a new society.

The author critically examines the views expressed in *Hind Swaraj*. It appears that *Hind Swaraj* did not receive much appreciation from the great scholars and the political leaders of India. W.J. Wybergh's criticism of *Hind Swaraj* in 1910 has the following points:

1. Liberation as the only goal would do more harm than good to the people of India at the cost of their desires and activities. By ignoring them there would be more stagnation and subjugation.
2. The concept of passive resistance suggested by Gandhi has its own ill-effects. It transfers the battle and violence from the physical plane to mental plane. Therefore, it is not spiritual at all.

3. Wybergh questions that whether "passive resistance" has anything to do with Christian conception of "non-resistance"? Of course, Gandhi replied to these objections by stating that his aim is to eliminate violence both from physical and mental realms.

The "lash of competition", according to Gandhi, does not increase the moral stature of any individual. Liberation as the immediate goal has to be in the mind of everyone although it may not be possible immediately. Looking back at *Hind Swaraj* after a century one would feel that Gandhi has certainly foreseen the dangerous consequences of modern civilization. The author asks whether we should read *Hind Swaraj* as a classic or as a manifesto of action? The author feels that it should be read as a classic work calling for reflection and reasoned action, and not only for arm chair reading.[3]

The author takes up Anthony J. Parel's introduction and interpretation of *Hind Swaraj*. Parel highlights the significance of the work and the intentions of Gandhi in writing this book. First of all, this book is a result of "inner illumination". Second, *swaraj* is strongly stamped on the minds of Indian people. Third, it aims at diverting the minds of Indian people from the violence of all sorts. Fourth, it aims at convincing people that modern civilization is the root cause of all social evils. Last, Gandhi's intention is to put forward a new political philosophy which is pragmatic and value oriented. Parel calls it "Gandhi's civic humanism". While analysing the historical context in which *Hind Swaraj* is written by Gandhi, Parel writes that Gandhi's critique of modern civilization is based on the philosophy of modern civilization which is rooted in the Enlightenment and the glorious Industrial Revolution of the West. Such a philosophy completely transformed the mindset of the Western people towards religion, ethics, knowledge,

---

[3] Pradhan 2011: 63.

phenomenal world and even the "other world". Life in the phenomenal world becomes more precious and there is a need to manage, manipulate and master it for satisfying human desires and aspirations. Industrial Revolution contributed to such a world-view by introducing machines that dominated human life. As a consequence, the phenomenal or everyday world was divided into civilized and non-civilized. The former represented the machine-dominated life of individuals and the latter, just opposite. This division further resulted in the establishment of colonial and imperial powers. This made British to establish colonial administration with absolute power to rule India. This is in this historical context that Gandhi opposed modern civilization. Parel further divides the intellectual context of *Hind Swaraj* into Western and Indian sources. The Western intellectuals like Anna Kingford, Howard Williams, Leo Tolstoy and John Ruskin inspired Gandhi a lot. The life of Christ and the "Sermon on the Mount" provided him with a sound spiritual background. As Parel puts it, Gandhi did not oppose Western civilization per se, but opposed modern civilization that has its roots in Enlightenment and industrialization. His critique of modern civilization is neither of parochialism nor cultural chauvinism. Similarly, Gandhi drew his inspiration from the theosophy of Anne Beasant and Madam Blavatsky. *Bhagavad-Gītā,* Buddha and Jainism provided him with ample spiritual base. The Jaina concept of Anekāntavāda (the many-sidedness of reality) helped Gandhi in shaping his own philosophy of praxis. Gandhi is completely convinced that there is no substitute to nonviolence. There is no scripture in this world that opposes this cardinal virtue. Parel sums up his work by stating that *Hind Swaraj* has contemporary relevance. The great Indian social reformers like Vinoba Bhave, Jayaprakash Narayan, Ram Manohar Lohia and many others successfully employed Gandhian ideals to achieve their ends.

III

This part deals with some key ideas of Gandhi. The author quotes from Gandhi to distinguish independence from *swaraj*.

> The word *swaraj* is a sacred word, a Vedic word, meaning self-rule and self-restraint, and freedom from all restraint which "independence" often means.[4]

The author raises an interesting question: Is Gandhi a proponent of pre-modernity, modernity or post-modernity? Where do we locate him? The author clarifies that pre-modernity stands for a set of cultural traits of a group or institution which remain from generation to generation without any radical change. On the contrary modernity stands for radical change in which there is a discontinuity with the past in terms of values, world-view, customs and technology and so on. Post-modernity is yet another intellectual movement which came into existence in the late twentieth century prompted by the great thinkers like Robert Venturi, Jean Baudrillard, Jean-Francois Lyotard, Jacques Derrida, Jean Bernard Leon Foucault, Michel Foucault, Jürgen Habermas and others. It departed from the modernist tradition which heavily relied on the grand narratives or theories or ideologies. It challenged the alleged claims of modernity of removing inequality, exploitation and domination. The epistemological tools of modernity and the role of scientific and objective knowledge are also questioned by the postmodernists. They never fixed the meaning of a text. To read a text means to trace the "process of constant flickering rather counting the beads in a necklace".

Gandhi's critique of modern civilization can be summed up in the following way:

1. Modern civilization is basically materialistic. The

---

[4] Pradhan 2011: 77.

hunger for wealth and worldly pleasures dominates human life.

2. Under modern civilization every individual becomes egocentric by looking for new avenues to become more affluent and to satisfy his/her desires.
3. The unhindered progress in the scientific and technology gradually deplete all natural resources. People are displaced from their natural habitat due to rapid developments in transportation and communications. Men are more interested in nurturing their animal appetites.

Such a critique of modernity by Gandhi makes us believe that he is a pre-modernist. Is it true? Many scholars are of the opinion that by opposing modern civilization Gandhi has taken us back to traditional value system. Of course, as aptly remarked by the author, it is not all that easy to explain the relation between tradition and modernity. There is a possibility of having "modernity of tradition" or "tradition of modernity". In other words, tradition becomes more elastic rather than being rigid. The age-old cultural symbols, myths and folklores are deeply rooted in the mindset of the people. When they are used with proper vision they can work out to be strong instruments of social change. Perhaps, Gandhi viewed traditional value system in this light. Gandhi was neither against science and technology nor interested in promoting traditional values at the cost of social change. As observed by the author, one has to understand Gandhian strategy only in the light of prevailing situation of his time. His critique is intended to make people of India aware that modern civilization in the lines of the British pattern would only damage the spirit of Indian freedom movement.

Another noted Gandhian scholar Bhikhu Parekh writes in his *Gandhi's Political Philosophy* that Gandhi's critique of modernity is completely different from that of the European critics. By being direct victims of modern civilization, both Gandhi and the people of India, could perceive the ill-effects of it more closely. Being ancient civilization one could see sensibility in the Indian civilization which is lacked in the modern civilization. Parekh also highlights the major positive sides of modern civilization as recognized by Gandhi. They are:

1. the spirit of inquiry and the search for truth,
2. bringing natural forces under human control, and
3. more organized social life.

But modern civilization failed to keep up proper balance among these three factors. Parekh observes that unfortunately the excesses committed by modern civilization perpetuated more evil by destroying good human life. At the same time Parekh points out three major setbacks of Gandhian critique of modern civilization. They are as follows:

1. Gandhi emphasized more on its negative side than its positive side. Modern civilization is not completely bereft of spiritual dimension in spite of the fact that its approach is rational.
2. Industrialization does not necessarily lead to colonialism and imperialism.
3. Gandhi looked at the positive side of modern civilization as an accident rather than an essential part of it.

But the author finds faults with Parekh's criticism of Gandhi's modern civilization on the following grounds. First of all, Parekh could not gauge the intentions of Gandhi when he criticized modern civilization. It hardly brought about any radical social change for the benefit of mankind. Second, Gandhi's critique of modern civilization has its own vantage point, namely, *daridranārāyaṇa.* Third, Gandhi's alternative to modern civilization cannot be easily dispensed with as otherwise believed by Parekh.

Coming to David Hardiman's critique of Gandhian critique of modernity in his *Gandhi: In His Time and Ours*, Hardiman argues that there is no fundamental difference between the value system proposed by Gandhi and that of modern civilization. In support of his argument, Hardiman recalls the statement made by Gandhi as early as in 1926 asking his countrymen to imbibe the ideas of the West, but advised them not to be indiscriminate in using them. Also, the views expressed in *Hind Swaraj*, maintains Hardiman, should not be taken literally. This is obvious from Gandhi's moderate views expressed in 1945 as regards the use of railways, hospitals and law courts. In fact, Gandhi's critique of materialistic and imperialistic use of science and technology takes us back to the debate between imperialistic science and Arcadian sensibility. The former makes use of science for the physical needs and pleasures while the latter looks at it for harmonious coexistence and purposeful human life. As Hardiman observes, Gandhi went beyond the Arcadian sensibility to approach nature with humility. The final submission of Hardiman is that Gandhi is not completely disillusioned by modernity.

Ramashray Roy observes in his *Self and Society and Gandhi: Sounding in Political Philosophy* that Gandhi's critique of modernity is completely different for Gandhi's world-view takes into account self-knowledge as the highest goal. Gandhi is also opposed to the expression "progress" which is the hallmark of modern civilization. The real progress for Gandhi lies in self-discovery. The paradigm shift that took place in the seventeenth century viewed man as autonomous and self-defining subject. This paved the way for a kind of social engineering wherein man-made institutions and natural order are used to serve the human purpose. Thus instrumental values gained upper hand over cardinal values. Roy also observes that Gandhi's critique of modern civilization is based on three important reasons:

1. Violence is in the very womb of modern civilization.
2. His critique of modern civilization is based on moral grounds.
3. Gandhi's critique is total and penetrating.

Therefore, Roy submits that Gandhi's critique of modern civilization ushers in an alternative and desirable society that suits the people of India.

Rudolphs-Lloyd's interpretation of Gandhi and post-modernism in his work *Postmodern Gandhi* co-authored with Susanne Rudolph highlights the following aspects. Gandhi's rejection of modernist expression "progress" makes him more a post-modernist rather than a traditionalist. Perhaps, he is one of the earliest post-modern writers who opposed the modernist view that epistemology rooted in scientific knowledge alone can result in universalism and objectivity. According to Rudolphs-Lloyd, Gandhi's views on relative truth perfectly fit into post-modernist scheme. Further, Gandhi rejected the traditional interpretation of the *Gītā* and followed his own interpretation of it. Thus one finds the post-modern hermeneutics in Gandhian interpretation. Gandhi did not merely reject the British rule which is rooted in modern civilization, but rejected the entire spectrum of modernity. According to the author, Rudolphs-Lloyd's attempt to find parallels between Gandhian conception of relative truth and post-modern conception of contingent truth is not appropriate. Unlike postmodernists, Gandhi did not support moral relativism. He is a firm believer in eternal truths and his attitude towards religion and morality cannot be compared with postmodernist view. The various interpretations presented by different scholars only suggest, according to the author, that Gandhian ideas are fertile.

The concepts of *swaraj* and *swadeshi* are the bedrocks of Gandhian philosophy. They served as a blueprint for preparing

Indian people for independence. These concepts also helped the Indian people to imagine independent India with a definite socio-economic, political and cultural structure. These concepts also enabled the people of India to transcend their national boundaries to visualize freedom at cosmic level. As a matter of fact, the expression *swaraj* is not the discovery of Gandhi. As a Vedic concept it popularly stood for self-rule. The British rule in India made this concept more vibrant than ever. Both the moderates and extremists of Indian National Congress accepted it, yet they did not use it in the same manner. For moderates it represented limited political freedom within the domain of the British rule. This is conspicuous in the address given by Dadabhai Naoroji at Calcutta Congress in 1906. For him the self-rule is nothing but self-government as followed in the other British colonies. But for extremists like Bipin Chandra Pal did not restrict *swaraj* to political and economic domains but also extended it to spiritual domain. Like Bipin Chandra Paul, Tilak viewed *swaraj* as a spiritual concept. Influenced by the *karma-yoga* of *Gītā* he held that:

> It is my conviction, it is my thesis that *swaraj* in the life to come cannot be a reward of the people who have not enjoyed it in this life.[5]

Although Tilak did not aim at absolute political independence of the country, he aimed at complete freedom to every individual in every aspect of social life. Tilak used the concept of *swaraj* to represent nationalism, democracy and spiritual freedom. The new dimensions added to *swaraj* by extremists are: boycott and *swadeshi*. These dimensions have also given new cultural twist to the people of India. The patriotic songs of Rabindranath Tagore, the art of Nand Lal Bose, the scientific temper of Jagadish Chandra Bose and P.C. Ray enthused and inspired the cultural life of the Indians.

---

5 Pradhan 2011: 102.

Gandhi's theory and practice of *swaraj* have their own distinctive features. After analysing the various debates associated with the concept of *swaraj* Gandhi thought true *swaraj* is possible only through nonviolence. Thus he is closer to the ideology of the moderates. However, Gandhi insisted that there must be the "reform of the soul" to achieve this great ideal. As the author rightly observes the chapters IV and XIV of *Hind Swaraj* are devoted to conceptualizing *swaraj* and the right means to achieve it. He opposed the hackneyed conception of *swaraj* and proposed a self-rule by ourselves. It is within us. As opposed to brute force, Gandhi proposed passive resistance as a means to achieve *swaraj*. The Garibaldian way of violence to free Italy from Austria is not a right means. Gandhi also adds new dimension to the concept of *swaraj*. They are:

1. national independence,
2. an all-inclusive nationhood,
3. people's right,
4. economic freedom,
5. the spiritual aspect of *swaraj*, and
6. duty before rights.

Without these components the concept of *swaraj* does not work well. Gandhi finally identifies *swaraj* with *Rāma-Rājya* wherein *dharma* or righteousness is given its due place. As it is held in the *Bible* "the Kingdom of God is within you". One who fights for *swaraj* must be free from base desires, according to Gandhi. It is the individual freedom that makes an individual completely devoted to the service of society. Of course, the author questions Gandhian notion of self-rule. How does one judge whether someone is "self-ruling" and free from base passions? There is no effective mechanism to find out one's inner experience. And extreme nationalism has its own dangers. Gandhi is aware of it. Extreme localism, jingoistic nationalism and woolly cosmopolitanism are not encouraged by Gandhi.

Satyāgraha: Theory and practice is another interesting chapter. Gandhi's study of *New Testament in Bible* and *Bhagavad-Gītā* laid firm foundation for his concept of *satyāgraha.* If an individual is interested in serving the society he must lead the life of purity and detachment. Gandhi's conviction in *satyāgraha* is further amplified by his reading of the "Sermon of the Mount" in the New Testament, *The Kingdom of God Within You* by Tolstoy and *Bhagavad-Gītā. Satyāgraha* means adherence to truth or insistence on truth. Gandhi used truth and God as synonyms. The force of love or the soul is more powerful than weapons. The power of *satyāgraha* would certainly yield the desired results, according to Gandhi. The Adviatic vision of Gandhi made him believe in the unity of all beings. Every individual has divinity within himself/herself. Thus Advaita served as a firm philosophical foundation for Gandhi. There is always a connection between the relative truths and the absolute truth. *Satyāgraha* is used as a weapon when all forms of dialogue come to an end. The interdependence between means and end is another philosophical foundation for *satyāgraha.* It is the means, believed Gandhi, that determine the end of any action. Gandhi's faith in the law of *karma* prompted him to believe in this causal link between means and end. *Satyāgraha* is a committed action to eradicate social evils such as untouchability, child marriage and so on. The forms of *satyāgraha* include:

1. persuasive *satyāgraha,*
2. *satyāgraha* through self-suffering,
3. individual *satyāgraha,*
4. mass *satyāgraha,*
5. non-cooperation,
6. strike,
7. hartal,

8. boycott, and
9. picketing.

Apart from that people may resort to non-cooperation, civil disobedience and open popular rebellion.

The author also tried to show the distinction between passive resistance and *satyāgraha.* According to him, Prahlāda in the Indian tradition and Socrates in the Greek tradition are known for their passive resistance. But in the case of *satyāgraha* there is no place for the enemy because an enemy becomes part and parcel of *satyāgraha* in the search for truth. The ideology of passive resistance is that it does not exclude physical force in the final eventuality. But *satyāgraha* does not encourage physical force at any level. Further, the author analyses Bhikhu Parekh's interpretation of *satyāgraha.* According to Parekh, Gandhi used *satyāgraha* the way in which it is understood in Gujarati. Even in Gujarati it is nothing but insistence on truth. For my part I do not find any fundamental difference between its use in Gujarati and Sanskrit. Parekh observes that Gandhi opposed prevailing methods of conflict resolution for they found wanting both in theoretical and practical respects. Mere appeal to rationality does not work well. One has to put one's heart and soul into it in order to promote mutual respect and goodwill. Since violence breads further violence, Gandhi resorted to nonviolence. Gandhi's departure from Kant and John Rawls, observes Parekh, regarding the nature justice is interesting. Gandhi, like ancient sages, would return good for evil to ensure moral impact of "suffering love". Gandhi advocated fasting only in extreme cases. However, Parekh sees limitations of *satyāgraha.* According to him, sometimes there is a genuine point of difference between a *satyāgrahī* and his opponents. The issues such as abortion, euthanasia and war cannot be settled amicably even on moral grounds. Parekh holds that it would be unimaginable to turn a stone-hearted Hitler into a compassionate human being. Gandhi failed to see the complex ways in which totalitarian regime demoralizes human beings. In his critical appreciation of *satyāgraha* the author considers the views of veteran freedom fighters like N.V. Gadgil and Vinoba Bhave. They hold that *satyāgraha* cannot be used against the democratically elected government where everything goes in accordance with the sovereign will of the people. But Ram Manohar Lohia, Jayaprakash Narayan, K. Santhanam and others felt that *satyāgraha* is the only sovereign remedy for protecting the human dignity. At the same time we need to assess the behaviour of our political representatives, for representative government is not always sacrosanct just because the majority accepted it. In order to protect the integrity of an individual or a group one can launch *satyāgraha*. Is *satyāgraha* a coercive method despite its nonviolent character? Arguments are made for and against *satyāgraha*. Can it be treated as a nonviolently violent act to blackmail the authorities to budge from their position? But the defenders of *satyāgraha* claim that it is violence against immoral practices. Some claim that *satyāgraha* is used as a successful method only in liberal democracies but not in all forms of government. Whether one would be successful or not in achieving his or his group's goal, it is the only legitimate method. From the incisive analysis provided by the author, it is clear that non-violent resistance which is the hallmark of a *satyāgrahī* has an edge over violent methods.

IV

This part deals with Gandhi and modern India. The issue of untouchability was one of the major challenges taken up by both Gandhi and Ambedkar. The fourfold division of the ancient Indian social order into brāhmaṇas, kṣatriyas, vaiśyas and śūdras has its merits and demerits. The *varṇa* system as advocated by the ancient Indian society is mainly intended to maintain a harmonious social order. The members of the each *varṇa* (social class) possess certain distinctive characteristics.

The *varṇa* system helps the society to maintain the division of labour. Of course, the sanctity of *varṇa* system could not be maintained in the course of historical social development since social classes are virtually turned into castes. The dominance of one social class over the other is challenged by the Buddhists and Jains. In fact, Gandhi supported the *varṇa* system. Although Gandhi claimed to be a *sanātanī* Hindu he sought radical reforms within Hinduism. He held that untouchability is a crime against humanity. One has to go beyond one's own body to see oneness of *ātman* in everyone. God being the creator of this universe one has to identify oneself with all living beings. One's love for others is exhibited through one's service to others. But what is unfortunate in the Indian spiritual tradition is that it did not give importance to manual labour. This was questioned by Gandhi. He reinterpreted *Gītā* to provide dignity to manual labour by holding that one who does not engage in manual work is a parasite and a thief. On the issue of untouchabililty there are differences between Gandhi and Ambedkar in spite of the fact they opposed it tooth and nail. Gandhi opposed untouchability as a crime against humanity but supported the *varṇa* system by reinterpreting it. On the contrary, Ambedkar vehemently opposed untouchability and claimed that the *varṇa* system is the root cause of this malady. Gandhi worked with Harijans and for their social and economic development. But Ambedkar was not happy with Gandhi because the latter turned it into a religious issue rather than a social one. Ambedkar castigated caste Hindus for perpetuating untouchability. One of the criticisms, according to author's observations, against Gandhi is that he could not grasp the socio-economic deprivations suffered by untouchables. He supported the *varṇa* system which is the root cause of this malady. But Ambedkar is also at fault on two counts. First of all, as a victim of *varṇa* system he vented his anger rather than trying to work out a strategy based on patience and perseverance. Also, the problem being an age-old one, cannot be settled overnight. However, both Gandhi and Ambedkar understood the Indian social system.

Coming to Gandhi, Muhammad Ali Jinnah, V.D. Savarkar and the Indian nationalism, Gandhi faced stiff opposition from both of them. Nationalism evokes strong patriotic feeling and national consciousness among the citizens of a country. It helps people to work for the development of their country. Indian nationalism is a peculiar phenomenon. It is an outcome of people belonging to different religions, regions, linguistic groups and so on. But what united them is their strong nationalism. Gandhi perceived that the cultural unity of India is the first step for the Indian nationalism. According to the author, the first contribution of Gandhi to the Indian nationalism is that he promoted religious tolerance. The existence of diverse religious groups was never a threat to the Indian nationalism. Religious freedom and secularism paved the way for such a unity among the people of India. The second contribution of Gandhi is the principle of non-violence. The nonviolent character of the Indian nationalism is another significant feature. It is only through "love-force" and "soul-force" we can attain our end. The third major contribution of Gandhi is that he tried to reconcile the Indian nationalism with internationalism and universalism. The Hindutva of Savarkar and the two nation theory of Jinnah are two major issues taken by the author in the context of Indian nationalism. Savarkar rejected Aryan invasion theory and claimed that Aryans were part of India. His preference for the expression "Hindutva" over "Hinduism" is based on the view that the former represents all the religious sects born out of the Indian soil, while the latter is simply restricted to a small section of people. On this basis he rejected the claims Indian Muslims and Indian Christians as part of the Hindu fold. The Hindu converts into Islam or Christianity are not treated as Hindus because their holy lands are outside

Hindustan. The parochial approach of M.S. Golwalker treated the Indian nation as the nation of Hindus alone.

On the contrary, the Indian Muslim League came out with its own structure of Indian nationalism. Although there was close interaction between Muslims and the Hindus it was in 1885 when the Indian National Congress was formed Sir Syed Ahmad Khan wanted his Muslim brethren to keep away from it. They demanded special status for Muslims in any political settlement in India. The divide between the Hindus and Muslims got further widened due to Ali brothers. Then it was Jinnah during the Lahore Conference held that Musalmans are a nation by themselves. They must have their own territory, homeland and state. Jinnah wanted the division of India on the basis of religious nationalism rather than on territorial basis as Muslims need their own identity. Finally Jinnah was successful in getting India partitioned. After becoming a separate state Jinnah was talking about civic nationalism in Pakistan. How could Gandhi face Savarkar and Golwalkar? As author rightly observes, Gandhi, Savarkar and Golwalkar have different views on Hinduism. Gandhi was a liberal Hindu with tolerance. But both Savarkar and Golwalkar were orthodox Hindus. In spite of Muslim support Gandhi could not avoid partition because of Jinnah's adamant behaviour. However, Jinnah was not a orthodox Muslim. Perhaps Jinnah was marginalized when Gandhi entered the picture. In order to make his own identity as a national figure he demanded separate state for Muslims. This is an interesting observation of the author. Thus Gandhi, Jinnah and Savarkar–Golwalkar represented civic, religious and ethnic forms of Indian nationalism, respectively.

Coming to Gandhi's approach to communal harmony, it is interesting to note that the mix up of religion with politics often leads to communal troubles. At least, there are four different reasons for that. They are:

1. domination of Church,
2. domination of the state,
3. separation of the Church and the state, and
4. their merger in a single institution/individual.

Gandhi worked a novel way through which religion and politics can be combined. The most important ingredient that balances both is morality. Religion as *dharma* has a vital role to play in politics. *Dharma* being eternal law enters into every aspect of human life. Gandhi viewed religion not in its narrower sense. Religion is that which binds people to truth. It is an element to be found in human nature. Such a view of religion transcends the historical religions. Gandhi visualized the same truth in all religions. He did not discriminate one religion against the other. Such a catholic approach to religions is the hallmark of Gandhian philosophy. Also he established firm link between religion and morality. They always sail together. A religious man is one who does not escape from the mundane world. He has to perform his duty for the sake of duty as highlighted in *Gītā*. Thus Gandhi felt that there is nothing wrong in making religion as a base for our politics. Gandhi's vision of politics is also based on the traditional value system. Politics is seen in every walk of life of an individual. Just as an individual demands for his rights, so also he has to take his duties as obligations. The citizens of a state are not only responsible for their own actions but also responsible for the actions of the state. If the state legislates a bad law, then they have to oppose it. Every spiritual-minded person must enter politics for the benefit of humanity. Gandhi viewed religion as a well-ordered moral government of the universe. Therefore, there is an inalienable relationship between religion and politics. Gandhi always pitched for secularism. But his secularism does not separate religion from politics as it is done in European secularism. He rejected the concept of power politics. Of course, Gandhi's views on religion and politics are viewed critically by many. According to Tilak, politics is the game of worldly people but not of *sādhus*. He did not undermine the role of morality and religion but he questioned their applicability in political arena. Jinnah's use of religion as a weapon to fulfil his political goal is questioned. Here it is clear that the interrelation between religion and politics is not a healthy combination. Politics, as indicated by the author, did not serve the cause of people in the post-Independent India. Gandhi believed that the sacred and the secular can go together.

Gandhi's view on the status of Indian women is another interesting issue taken up by the author with a critical eye. Unfortunately the women in the Indian tradition are deprived of *mokṣa* like the śūdras. Traditional Indian women are confined to the four walls of the home. They do not share any public space with men. But the situation gradually changed over a period of time. But in the Vedic era women enjoyed equal status with men. Maitreyī, the wife of Yājñavalkya, could debate with him on mundane and extra-mundane issues. There were many such instances in the history of Indian tradition. On the contrary, in the *Manu-Smṛti* women are always put in the custody of a male member. Thus it lowered the status of women. Gandhi was deeply concerned with the status of Indian women in the society. Gandhi cited his own mother as an ideal for womanhood. He did not differentiate the role of women from that of men. Gandhi never felt one gender is inferior to the other. At the same time, Gandhi, unlike the modern feminists, refused to abolish gender difference. For him, the gender difference has its own role to play. The genders are complimentary and supplementary in social life. The role of women and men in the society is clearly demarcated. What is possible for women is not possible for men and vice versa. The roles played by women and men should not affect the gender equality, according to Gandhi. The social evils like wearing *purdah*, child marriages and forced widowhood must be opposed for the better status of women in the society. By granting freedom to women Gandhi envisaged that divorce is welcome if a woman's freedom is under threat. *Devadāsī* system and the institution of prostitution should be abolished. He went to an extent of advising people that conjugal life is for mere procreation but not for recreation. Of course, Gandhi's views on the Indian women are subjected to criticism. Patriarchy is the chief villain of the piece. It is perpetuated by Gandhi even in his *āśrama*. He led the national movement as a patriarch. Gandhi was insensitive to women sexuality and their sexual desires.

Finally, a critical appreciation of Gandhian thought would bring this present work to an end. The author observes that the seminal point on which Gandhian political philosophy hangs is the symbiotic relation between man and his fellow beings and nature. As a follower of Advaita tradition Gandhi felt that self-transformation destroys all dichotomies which are the creation of *avidyā*. In his secular perspective, Gandhi tried to see religion and politics interdependent. His theory and practice of nonviolence is another important milestone in the human history. His theory and practice of *satyāgraha* is another important contribution of Gandhi to social humanism. Gandhi's moral critique of modern civilization must be taken in its right spirit. In spite of vehement criticism from different quarters Gandhi remained as one of the strongest national leaders who led the Indian masses towards freedom.

V

In this part the author quotes the most interesting and inspiring sayings of Gandhi on the issues such as meaning of *swaraj*, in defence of nationalism, India's cultural heritage, regeneration of Indian women, women's education, communal unity, the curse of untouchability, religious tolerance in India, the problem of minorities.

From the perspective of the reviewer, the author has done an excellent job in providing historical, analytical and evaluative dimensions of Gandhian thought along with his own interpretation of it. I deliberately converted this review into a review article for I had to cover all the important dimensions of the present work for the benefit of the readers.

Epilogue

To sum up, Gandhian idealism has both positive and negative sides. Idealism per se is not dangerous for it regulates unhealthy practices of individuals by reminding them of their social responsibilities as members of any civil society. The robust idealism of Gandhi encompasses nonviolence, compassion and love as its constitutive features. The philosophy of *satyāgaraha* which is the backbone of Gandhian idealism advocates that we can conquer injustice by our passionate adherence to truth. It certainly worked when Gandhi was leading the masses. But Gandhi did not expect that the world in which we live at present is what he expected it to be. The application of such robust idealism in social, political and international levels of action is not all that easy for the individuals are failing to realize the primacy of needs over wants and duties over rights. Thus the success of Gandhian idealism requires many provisos.

Practising idealism at individual level is not a problem. But its application at the collective level is not going to be a successful venture. Gandhian idealism has certain limitations imposed on its effectiveness due to the changing nature of man, society and politics. The debunk value system is the root cause of all social maladies. Rapid industrialization led to the establishment of soft-totalitarian societies which reduced individuals to the level of consumers. These societies have enacted their own (material) values wherein commodity fetishism reigns supreme. In such societies individuals gradually lose their social identity and become tools in the production process. Life becomes mechanical and there would be no time for creativity. The capabilities of individuals are neglected and their brute capacities are used for the production process. Quantitative aspects of human life get more priority than the qualitative ones. Sense of participation of individuals gets minimized and machinery overwhelms human resources. These are the negative aspects of extreme form of modernization. Anticipating such a state of dehumanization Gandhi often warned us not to neglect tradition and culture which keep human values intact.

Tradition and culture guided the societies in the past and are guiding them at present by reminding humans of their social responsibilities. Just as societies are evolving, tradition and culture too evolve. Blind habits and slavish obedience to any authority have to be questioned. This is where reason comes into picture. As Immanuel Kant rightly observed, pure reason has its limitations. Formal or pure reason become highly theoretical and practical reason has to come into play to establish non-material values such as freedom, morality and religion. But the ideals of progress need not be always the products of discursive thought. This is what Gandhi reminded us time and again. Scientific realism and moral or philosophical idealism have to be combined together to make our ideals concrete and realizable. For instance, rapid industrialization has led to global warming. All of us are concerned with it, but have no commitment to minimize it. What Gandhi would suggest to all of us to minimize this global warming is to bring about a change in our lifestyle.

We have right to make use of the bounty of nature without destroying its very existence. We destroy its very existence by wasting the products of nature. We cannot afford to eat more than what we can chew. Preservation of life and the furtherance of quality of life on the globe have to be our first priority. Like the Buddha and Aristotle, Gandhi advised us to tread a middle path in order to protect human values on the one hand and to promote science and technology on the other. Gandhi was also aware of the negative side of the tradition. Blind adherence to tradition without questioning its legitimacy is also dangerous. The divisive and the destructive features of tradition have to be identified and shunned. Similar is the case with modernity. What is conducive for the quality of life has to be imbibed, and those elements which rob human life of its quality have to be thrown overboard. Gandhi's appeal to all of us is to maintain a balanced approach to promote tradition as well as modernity.

The critics of Gandhi often brand him as a moral puritan, reactionary and a moral fanatic. Such attacks on Gandhi are ill-tempered. Gandhi firmly believed that what is morally right would be the most effective course of conduct in the public sphere. Although Gandhi derived his values from certain metaphysical presuppositions he always believed in putting them to pragmatic tests. Therefore, it is the primacy of practical reason over pure reason that dominates Gandhian thought. Of course, we need to be modest in accepting that everything that is advocated by Gandhi may not work all the time like a talisman. The changing times need new strategies. This is where I compare Gandhi with critical theorists. He never held that his principles are immune to revision. He was highly self-critical. However, the cardinal virtues of Gandhian thought (nonviolence, adherence to truth, compassion and love) remain as the guiding principles of our actions.

Bibliography

Primary Sources

Gandhi, M.K., 1959, *Hind Swaraj*, Ahmedabad: Navajivan Publishing House.

———, 1962, *My Experiments with Truth*, Ahmedabad: Navajivan Publishing House.

Secondary Sources

Balasubramanian, R., 1991, "The Hindu Attitude to Knowledge and Nature", in Ravi Ravindra (ed.) *Sceince and Spirit*, New York: Paragon House.

Bondurant, Joan V., 1958, *Conquest of Violence: The Gandhian Philosophy of Conflict*, New Jersey: Princeton University Press.

Bose, N.K., 1972, *Selections from Gandhi*, Ahmedabad: Navajivan Publishing House.

Brecher, Michael, 1996, "Crisis, Conflict, War: State of the Discipline", *International Political Science Review*, **17**(2).

Chatterjee, Margaret, 1983, *Gandhi's Religious Thought*, London: Macmillan.

Cole, Darrell, 2005-06, "Review of Juergensmeyer's Gandhi's Way: A Hand Book of Conflict Resolution", *Journal of Law and Religion*, **XXI**(1): 197-200.

Das. A., 1979, "Gandhian Critique of Modern Economic Theory", *Gandhi Marg*, **39**: 327.

Dutta, D.M., 1953, *The Philosophy of Mahatma Gandhi*, Wisconsin: The University of Wisconsin Press.

Erikson, Erik H., 1970, *Gandhi's Truth*, London: Faber & Faber.

Fischer, Louis, 1957, *The Life of Mahatma Gandhi*, London: Jonathan Cape.

Gandhi, M.K., 1933, *Speeches and Writings of Mahatma Gandhi*, Madras: G.A. Natesan & CO., 4th edn.

———, 1944, *Constructive Programme*, Ahmedabad: Navajivan Press.

———, 1951, *Satyagraha*, Ahmedabad: Navajivan Publishing House.

Gangal, Anurag, 1985, *New International Economic Order: Gandhian Perspective*, New Delhi: Advent Books.

Ganguli, B.N., 1973, *Gandhi's Social Philosophy: Perspective and Relevance*, Delhi: Vikas Publishing House Pvt. Ltd.

Gene, Sharp, 1979, *Gandhi as a Political Strategist*, Boston: Porter Sargent Publishers Inc.

Gora, 1951, *An Atheist with Gandhi*, Ahmedabad: Navajivan Publishing House.

Gregg, Richard B., 1960, *The Power of Non-Violence*, Ahmedabad: Navajivan Publishing House, preface.

———, 1960, "The Power of Gandhi's Non-Violence", in his *Profiles of Gandhi*, New York: IBC.

Guha, Ramachndra, 2007, *India After Gandhi: The History of the World's Largest Democracy*, London: Harper and Collins.

Iyer, Raghvan, 1983, *The Moral and Political Thought of Gandhi*, New York: Concord Grove Press.

Juergensmeyer, Mark, 2005, *Gandhi's Way: A Hand Book of Conflict Resolution*, California: University of California Press.

Koller, John M., 1970, *Oriental Philosophies*, New York: Charles Scribners' Sons.

Kripalani, J.B., 1953, *The Gandhian Way*, New Delhi: Publications Division.

Kumarappa, B. (ed.), 1951, *Towards Non-Violent Socialism*, Ahmedabad: Navajivan Publishing House.

——— (ed.), 1958-84, *Collected Works of Mahatma Gandhi*, Ahmedabad: Navajivan Trust.

Lenin, 1917, *Collected Works*, vols. 1. and 25, Moscow: Progress Publishers.

Manin, Ethel, 2006, "The Power of Non-Violence", in *Mahatma Gandhi: Essays and Reflections*, ed. S. Radhakrishnan, Mumbai, Kolkota, Delhi: Jaico Publishing.

Marx, Karl, 1867, *Das Capital*, vol. 1, Moscow: Progress Publishers.

———, 1875, *Critique of the Gotha Programme: Marx and Engels, Selected Works*, Moscow: Progress Publishers, vol. 3.

Misra, K.P.,1981, *Gandhi and the Contemporary World*, Delhi: Chanakya Publications.

Murty, K.S., 1965, *The Indian Spirit*, Waltair: Andhra University Press.

———, 1982, *Indian Philosophy Since 1948*, Visakhapatnam: Aruna Press.

Parekh, Bhikhu, 1989, *Colonialism, Tradition and Reform: An Analysis of Gandhi's Political Discourse*, New York: Sage Publishers.

———, 1991, *Gandhi's Political Philosophy*, London: Palgrave Macmillan.

———, 2001, *Gandhi: A Very Short Introduction*, London: Oxford University Press.

Pradhan, Ram Chandra, 2011, *Reading and Reappraising Gandhi*, New Delhi: Macmillan.

Radhakrishnan, S., 1958, "Gandhi: The Practical Idealist", in *All Men Are Brothers: A Selection of Mahatma's Writings*, Paris: UNESCO Publication.

———, (ed.), 1977, *Mahatma Gandhi: Essays and Reflections on His Life and Work*, Bombay: Jaico Press Pvt. Ltd.

Raju, P.T., 1985, *Structural Depths of Indian Thought*, New Delhi: South Asian Publishers.

Ray, Niharranjan, (ed.), 1969, *Gandhi: Theory and Practice, Impact, and Contemporary Relevance*, Shimla: Indian Institute of Advanced Study.

Ray, Sibnarayan, *Gandhi: India and the World*, Bombay: Nachiketa Publication Ltd., 1970.

Schumacher, E.F., 1973, *Small Is Beautiful: A Study of Economics as if People Mattered*, London: Blond and Briggs.

Sethi, J.D., 1979, *Gandhi Today*, New Delhi: Vikas Publishers.

Sharma, Chandradhar, 1979, *A Critical Survey of Indian Philosophy*, Delhi: Motilal Banarsidass, repr.

Singh, Ramjee, 1988, *Gandhi and the Modern World*, New Delhi: Classical Publishing Company.

Subramanyam, V.K., 1980, *Maxims of Chanakya*, New Delhi: Abhinav Publication.

Index

ahimsā, 81
Ambedkar, B.R., 105-07
anekāntavāda, 95
aparigraha, 56
Apollonians, 8
Aristotle, 7, 58, 114
artha 52-55
Arthaśāstra 53
Aśoka, 37
ātman, 55, 106
Aurobindo, Sri, 9, 58
Austin, John Langshaw, 91
avidyā, 26

Balasubramanian, R., 53
Ball, Terence, 88-89, 91-92
Baudrillard, Jean, 96
Beasant, Anne, 95
Behme, Jacob, 25
Bhagavad-Gītā, 18-19, 27, 92, 95, 100-01, 109
bhāṣyakāras, 89
Bhave, Vonoba, 95, 105
Bible, 7, 102
Blavetsky, Helena, 95
Bose, Jagdish Chandra, 101
Bose, Nand Lal, 101
Brecher, Michael, 42
Buddha, 114
Buddhism, 95
Bunyan, John, 25

Chomsky, Noam, 5
Christ, Jesus, 16, 39, 77, 95
Christianity, 77
Cole, Darrell, 44-45

daridranārāyaṇa, 98
Darwin, Charles, 14
Derrida, Jacques, 96
Descartes, Renë, 13
devadāsī, 111
dharma, 30, 37, 51-55, 102, 109
Dionysians, 8

Eckhart, Meister, 25

Einstein, Albert, 41
Engels, Frederick, 85

freedom, 9-10, 20, 38, 72
Foucault, Jean Bernard Leon, 96
Foucault, Michel, 96

Gadamer, Hans-Georg, 91
Gadgil, N.V., 105
Gandhi, Mohandas Karamchand, 1-25, 27-32, 34, 36-46, 48, 51, 55-57, 61, 64-67, 69-72, 74-82, 86-88, 92-100, 102-11, 113-15
Gangal, Anurag, 42
God, 6, 10-13, 30, 32, 37, 106
Golwalker, M.S., 108
Greenberg, Hayim, 46
Gregg, Richard B., 40-41
guṇas, 50

Habermas, Jürgen, 91, 96
Hardiman, David, 99
Heidegger, Martin, 17, 91
Hindu(s), 30-31, 52, 93, 108
Hinduism, 106
Hitler, Adolf, 29

Jainism, 17, 95
Jews, 45-46
Jinnah, Muhammad Ali, 107-08
Juergensmeyer, Mark, 43-45

kāma, 52, 54-55
Kāmasūtra, 54
Kant, Immanuel, 2-3, 114
karmayogī, 1
Kauṭilya, 25, 52
Khan, Sir Syed Ahmad, 108
Kingford, Anna, 95
Koller, John M., 5, 53
Kumarappa, Bharatan, 42

Lloyd, Rudolphs, 100
Locke, John, 5, 48
Lohia, Ram Manohar, 95, 105
love, 10, 13
Lyotard, Jean-Francois, 96

Mahābhārata, 52-54
Mandela, Nelson, 41
Manin, Ethel, 37
Manu, 52, 54
Marx, Karl, 7, 22, 75-76, 80, 82-87
Mashruwala, Kishore Lal, 64
Minogue, Kenneth, 91
mokṣa, 52, 55
Murty, K.S., 65

Muslim(s), 31, 93, 107-08
mysticism 3

Naoroji, Dadabhai, 101
Narayan, Jayaprakash, 95, 105
Nationalism, Indian, 93, 107
Nazis, 45-46
Neibuhr, Reinhold, 45
Nietzsche, Fredrick, 8
nonviolence, 11, 14-15, 17, 20, 28, 30, 36-41, 64, 73, 81, 115
noumenal, 26

Pañcatantra, 53-54
Parekh, Bikkhu, 97-98, 104
Parel, Anthony J., 94-95
Parikh, Narahari, 64
Pascal, Blaise, 25
Paul, Bipin Chandra, 101
peace, 24, 28
phenomenal, 26, 95
philosophy, Gandhian, 1-2, 28, 31, 61-63, 109
Plato, 50
Pradhan, Ram Chandra, 88, 94
Purdah, 111
puruṣārthas, 52

Radhakrishnan, Sarvepalli, 28, 41

rajas, 50
Rāma-Rājya, 21, 102
Rāmāyaṇa, 92
Rawls, John, 104
Ray, P.C., 101
religion, 12, 24, 26, 69, 100, 109-10
Rousseau, Jean-Jacques, 48
Roy, Ramashray, 99
ṛta, 12
Ruskin, John, 67, 95

Śaṅkara, 1
Santhanam, K., 105
Sartre, Jean-Paul, 20
Sarvodaya, 80
sattva, 50
satyāgraha, 14, 29, 30, 45, 65, 103-05, 111, 113
Savarkar, Vinayak Damodar, 107-08
Sen, Amartya, 59
Sermon on Mount, 95
Sharma, Chandradhara, 54
Silpa Archa, 49
Skinner, Quentin, 88, 90
Skolimowsky, Henryk, 21
Socrates, 9, 28
spirituality, 24-25, 27
St. Francis of Assisi, 25

St. John of the Cross, 25
Strauss, Leo, 89-91
swadeshi, 43, 100-01
swarāj, 93, 100-02, 111

Tagore, Rabindranath, 101
tamas, 50
Thoreau, Henry David, 7
Tilak, Bal Gangadhar, 101
Tolstoy, Leo, 7, 67, 95
trusteeship, 62-65, 76
truth, 6, 13, 19, 29, 30, 37, 40,100

Upaniṣads, 55
utilitarianism, 80
values, 47, 50-51, 55-59, 69, 72, 78, 86, 99
varṇa, 51, 105-06
Vātsāyana, 54
Ventury, Robert, 96

Williams, Howard, 95
Wittgenstein, Ludwig, 32
Wybergh, W.J., 93, 94